Children Celebrate

Harry Langdon

Children Celebrate:
39 Plays for Feasts

St.
Anthony
Messenger
Press

CINCINNATI, OHIO

Nihil Obstat: Rev. Hilarion Kistner, O.F.M.
Rev. Robert J. Buschmiller

Imprimi Potest: Rev. John Bok, O.F.M.
Provincial

Imprimatur: Rev. R. Daniel Conlon
Chancellor and Vicar General
Archdiocese of Cincinnati
November 17, 1992

The *nihil obstat* and *imprimatur* are a declaration that a book is considered to be free from doctrinal or moral error. It is not implied that those who have granted the *nihil obstat* and *imprimatur* agree with the contents, opinions or statements expressed.

Cover and book design by Julie Lonneman
Cover illustration by Mary Beth Owens

ISBN 0-86716-165-5

Published by St. Anthony Messenger Press
Printed in the U.S.A.

Contents

Annual Feast Days (U.S.A.)

This calendar of feasts will help you find the play best suited for a particular feast or special anniversary or for the type of community (e.g., martyrs, bishops, priests) to which a particular saint belongs or the type of event in Christ's life.

Feast Days With Nonvarying Calendar Dates

Date	Feast	Play(s)	Page
January			
1	Solemnity of Mary, Mother of God	1 or 33	3 or 73
2	St. Basil the Great and St. Gregory Nazianzen, bishops and doctors	27 or 29	59 or 63
5	St. John Neumann, bishop	27	59
6	Epiphany of the Lord	1	3
7	St. Raymond of Penyafort, priest	34	75
13	St. Hilary, bishop and doctor	27 or 29	59 or 63
17	St. Anthony, abbot	34	75
20	St. Fabian, pope and martyr	32 or 36	70 or 79
	St. Sebastian, martyr	32	70
21	St. Agnes, virgin and martyr	32 or 39	70 or 85
22	St. Vincent, deacon and martyr	32	70
24	St. Francis de Sales, bishop and doctor	27 or 29	59 or 63
25	Conversion of St. Paul, apostle	2	6
26	St. Timothy and St. Titus, bishops	27	59
27	St. Angela Merici, virgin	39	85
28	St. Thomas Aquinas, priest and doctor	29 or 34	63 or 75
31	St. John Bosco, priest	34	9 or 75

February

March

April

23	St. George, martyr	32	70
24	St. Fidelis of Sigmaringen, priest and martyr	32 or 34	70 or 75
25	St. Mark, evangelist	10	25
28	St. Peter Chanel, priest and martyr	32 or 34	70 or 75
29	St. Catherine of Siena, virgin and doctor	29 or 39	63 or 85
30	St. Pius V, pope	36	79

May

1	St. Joseph the Worker	8	21
2	St. Athanasius, bishop and doctor	27 or 29	59 or 63
3	St. Philip and St. James, apostles	25	53
12	St. Nereus and St. Achilleus, martyrs	32	70
	St. Pancras, martyr	32	70
14	St. Matthias, apostle	25	53
15	St. Isidore the Farmer	37	81
18	St. John I, pope and martyr	32 or 36	70 or 79
20	St. Bernardine of Siena, priest	34	75
25	St. Bede, priest and doctor	29 or 34	63 or 75
	St. Gregory VII, pope	36	79
	St. Mary Magdalene de Pazzi, virgin	39	85
26	St. Philip Neri, priest	34	75
27	St. Augustine of Canterbury, bishop	27	59
31	Visitation of Our Lady	33	73

June

1	St. Justin, martyr	32	70
2	St. Marcellinus and St. Peter, martyrs	32	70
3	St. Charles Lwanga and companions, martyrs	32	70
5	St. Boniface, bishop and martyr	27 or 32	59 or 70
6	St. Norbert, bishop	27	59
7	Immaculate Heart of Mary	33	73
9	St. Ephrem, deacon and doctor	29	63
11	St. Barnabas, apostle	25	53
13	St. Anthony of Padua, priest and doctor	29 or 34	63 or 75
19	St. Romuald, abbot	34	75
21	St. Aloysius Gonzaga, religious	37	81

22	St. Paulinus of Nola, bishop	27	59
	St. Thomas More, martyr	32	70
	St. John Fisher, bishop and martyr	27 or 32	59 or 70
24	Birth of St. John the Baptist	11	27
27	St. Cyril of Alexandria, bishop and doctor	27 or 29	59 or 63
28	St. Irenaeus, bishop and martyr	27 or 32	59 or 70
29	St. Peter and St. Paul, apostles	25	53
30	First Martyrs of the Roman Church	32	70

July

3	St. Thomas, apostle	25	53
4	St. Elizabeth of Portugal	37	81
5	St. Anthony Zaccaria, priest	34	75
6	St. Maria Goretti, virgin and martyr	32 or 39	70 or 85
11	St. Benedict, abbot	12	29
13	St. Henry	37	81
14	Blessed Kateri Tekakwitha, virgin	39	85
	St. Camillus de Lellis, priest	34	75
15	St. Bonaventure, bishop and doctor	27 or 29	59 or 63
16	Our Lady of Mount Carmel	33	73
21	St. Lawrence of Brindisi, priest and doctor	29 or 34	63 or 75
22	St. Mary Magdalene	37	81
23	St. Bridget, religious	37	81
25	St. James, apostle	25	53
26	St. Joachim and St. Ann, parents of Mary	37	81
29	St. Martha	37	81
30	St. Peter Chrysologus, bishop and doctor	27 or 29	59 or 63
31	St. Ignatius of Loyola, priest	13	31

August

1	St. Alphonsus Liguori, bishop and doctor	14	33
2	St. Eusebius of Vercelli, bishop	27	59
4	St. John Vianney, priest	34	75
5	Dedication of St. Mary Major	33	73
6	Transfiguration of the Lord	15	35

7	St. Sixtus II, pope and martyr, and companions, martyrs	32 or 36	70 or 79
	St. Cajetan, priest	34	75
8	St. Dominic, priest	34	75
10	St. Lawrence, deacon and martyr	32	70
11	St. Clare, virgin	39	85
13	St. Pontian, pope and martyr	32 or 36	70 or 79
	St. Hippolytus, priest and martyr	32 or 34	70 or 75
14	St. Maximilian Mary Kolbe, priest and martyr	32 or 34	70 or 75
15	Assumption of Our Lady	33	73
16	St. Stephen of Hungary	37	81
18	St. Jane Frances de Chantal	37	81
19	St. John Eudes, priest	34	75
20	St. Bernard, abbot and doctor	29	63
21	St. Pius X, pope	36	79
22	Queenship of Mary	33	73
23	St. Rose of Lima, virgin	39	85
24	St. Bartholomew, apostle	25	53
25	St. Louis	37	81
	St. Joseph Calasanz, priest	34	75
27	St. Monica	37	81
28	St. Augustine, bishop and doctor	27 or 29	59 or 63
29	Beheading of St. John the Baptist, martyr	11 or 32	27 or 70

September

3	St. Gregory the Great, pope and doctor	29 or 36	63 or 79
8	Birth of Mary	33	73
9	St. Peter Claver, priest	34	75
13	St. John Chrysostom, bishop and doctor	27 or 29	59 or 63
14	Triumph of the Cross	16	37
15	Our Lady of Sorrows	33	73
16	St. Cornelius, pope and martyr	32 or 36	70 or 79
	St. Cyprian, bishop and martyr	27 or 32	59 or 70
17	St. Robert Bellarmine, bishop and doctor	27 or 29	59 or 63
19	St. Januarius, bishop and martyr	27 or 32	59 or 70
21	St. Matthew, apostle and evangelist	25	53
26	St. Cosmas and St. Damian, martyrs	32	70

27	St. Vincent de Paul, priest	34	75
28	St. Wenceslaus, martyr	32	70
	St. Lawrence Ruiz and companions, martyrs	32	70
29	Sts. Michael, Gabriel and Raphael, archangels	24	51
30	St. Jerome, priest and doctor	29 or 34	63 or 75

October

1	St. Theresa of the Child Jesus, virgin	39	85
2	Guardian Angels	24	51
4	St. Francis of Assisi	17	39
6	St. Bruno, priest	34	75
	Blessed Marie-Rose Durocher, religious	37	81
7	Our Lady of the Rosary	33	73
9	St. Denis, bishop and martyr, and companions, martyrs	27 or 32	59 or 70
14	St. Callistus I, pope and martyr	32 or 36	70 or 79
15	St. Teresa of Avila, virgin and doctor	18	41
16	St. Hedwig, religious	37	81
	St. Margaret Mary Alacoque, virgin	38 or 39	83 or 85
17	St. Ignatius of Antioch, bishop and martyr	27 or 32	59 or 70
18	St. Luke, evangelist	19	42
19	St. Isaac Jogues and St. John de Brebeuf, priests and martyrs, and companions, martyrs	32 or 34	70 or 75
23	St. John of Capistrano, priest	34	75
24	St. Anthony Claret, bishop	27	59
28	St. Simon and St. Jude, apostles	25	53

November

1	All Saints	20	43
2	All Souls	20	43
3	St. Martin de Porres, religious	21	45
4	St. Charles Borromeo, bishop	27	59
9	Dedication of St. John Lateran	25 or 36	53 or 79
10	St. Leo the Great, pope and doctor	29 or 36	63 or 79
11	St. Martin of Tours, bishop	27	59
12	St. Josaphat, bishop and martyr	27 or 32	59 or 70
13	St. Frances Xavier Cabrini, virgin	39	85

15	St. Albert the Great, bishop and doctor	27 or 29	59 or 63
16	St. Margaret of Scotland	37	81
	St. Gertrude, virgin	39	85
17	St. Elizabeth of Hungary, religious	37	81
18	Dedication of Sts. Peter and Paul	25	53
	St. Rose Philippine Duchesne, virgin	39	85
21	Presentation of Mary	33	73
22	St. Cecilia, virgin and martyr	32 or 39	70 or 85
23	St. Clement I, pope and martyr	32 or 36	70 or 79
	St. Columban, abbot	34	75
30	St. Andrew, apostle	25	53

December

3	St. Francis Xavier, priest	13	31
4	St. John Damascene, priest and doctor	29 or 34	63 or 75
6	St. Nicholas, bishop	22	47
7	St. Ambrose, bishop and doctor	27 or 29	59 or 63
8	Immaculate Conception	33	73
11	St. Damascus I, pope	36	79
12	Our Lady of Guadalupe	23	49
13	St. Lucy, virgin and martyr	32 or 39	70 or 85
14	St. John of the Cross, priest and doctor	18	41
21	St. Peter Canisius, priest and doctor	29 or 34	63 or 75
23	St. John of Kanty, priest	34	75
25	Christmas	1	3
26	St. Stephen, first martyr	32	70
27	St. John, apostle and evangelist	25	53
28	Holy Innocents, martyrs	32	70
29	St. Thomas Becket, bishop and martyr	27 or 32	59 or 70
31	St. Sylvester I, pope	36	79

Feast Days With Varying Calendar Dates

Introduction

Over ten years ago, my family and I lived in Dodge City, Kansas. One of my many fond memories of life there was children's drama in weekday liturgies at the Cathedral of the Sacred Heart School. The plays were directed and supported by the Sisters of St. Joseph of Wichita, women with whom I taught at St. Mary of the Plains College.

Hence, my positive experience with in-school liturgical drama inspired this book, a successor to *Twenty-six Biblical Playlets for Learning and Liturgy* (Liguori, Mo.: Liguori Publications, 1988). *Children Celebrate* is a second collection of plays for use in liturgical services or religious education programs. Whereas the focus of *Twenty-six Biblical Playlets for Learning and Liturgy* was on familiar Scripture passages for weekend liturgies, the focus of this book is on the saints of the Church as they are honored throughout the liturgical year. Also included are plays for honoring beatified persons and for Church feasts. These plays can be performed during school Masses, at school assemblies or in the classroom. Some plays honor a group such as pastors, angels, virgins, holy persons or religious women rather than one person. A calendar of Church feast days suggests which plays to use for which feasts.

In the liturgy of the Mass, as outlined in the *Directory for Masses With Children* (paragraph 47), the plays could be presented in the homily or in the form of a commentary before the Scripture readings. They might also serve as an entrance ceremony as well as a communion meditation.

Liturgical planners should keep in mind that the *Directory* is very clear about Scripture readings being proclaimed without using paraphrase (paragraphs 41-45). Masses with children such as those celebrated during the schoolday are supposed to lead children to full participation in the celebration of the Eucharist with the entire community on Sunday. Hence, children's Masses must not be radically different from those of the parish community. Otherwise, the catechetical value of initiation into the larger community is lost (*Directory*, paragraph 21). Planners, then, need to be prudent in their pastoral judgment when trying to be creative with the Eucharist.

Major Sunday feasts such as Christ the King, Easter and Pentecost, should be celebrated on Sunday with the parish.

Within the religion lesson, the plays can be used as springboards for discussing the meaning of the saint's life and the application of this meaning to our lives today.

Although the plays have been primarily designed for young people, they may be performed by adults or mixed casts of adults and children. They may also serve as models for creating original plays about the saints not included in this collection.

1.
January 1: Solemnity of Mary, Mother of God

Note: This play can also be used for the Feast of the Holy Family or the Feast of the Epiphany.

Cast of characters:
    YOUNG MARY
    OLDER MARY
    JESUS, age 12
    JOSEPH THE OLDER
    JOSEPH THE YOUNGER
    KING ONE, KING TWO and KING THREE

Props needed: Short tunic or piece of cloth that the OLDER MARY is sewing. A piece of wood and cloth for JESUS. JOSEPH with a piece of wood identical in size and appearance to JESUS' piece. YOUNG MARY holds a doll representing the Christ Child. There should be a stool at stage left on which the YOUNG MARY can sit. KING ONE carries a rich-looking sack for the gold; KING TWO holds a censer full of incense; KING THREE brings a perfume bottle.

Music: "We Three Kings"

> (*The OLDER MARY enters from right sewing a short tunic belonging to JESUS, who follows her. He is about twelve. JESUS is polishing a piece of wood with a cloth.*)

THE OLDER MARY: Jesus, I don't understand how you get so many holes in your clothes.

JESUS: Oh, I snag them on the tools in Dad's workshop.

MARY: You really should be more careful in the workshop. I worry about you sometimes, especially when you wander off—like you did at the Passover festival in Jerusalem.

JESUS: But, Mom, I have to speak to the priests and elders at the Temple.

MARY: My son, Joseph and I have always had trouble understanding all the messages you and we have received from God. But since we love and trust you, we know you can speak only the truth.

(JOSEPH enters with his piece of wood—exactly the same in size as the one JESUS has. He is looking for JESUS, calling his name.)

JOSEPH: Jesus! Ah, there you are. I wanted to check to see if this board was the same size as yours. *(They compare the boards.)*

JESUS: I'm sure they are, Dad. I checked them earlier.

JOSEPH: Good! I'm trying to repair a cabinet, you know, the one that your Mother and I received when you were born. One of the doors is broken. It's the cabinet that holds the gold, frankincense and myrrh that the three kings from the East brought to you when you were born.

(MARY walks over to join JESUS and JOSEPH at stage right and puts her arms around JESUS.)

MARY: I can still remember, Jesus, how amazed your father and I were when those great men came to the stable with those precious gifts. *(The YOUNG MARY comes slowly from the left to sit on a stool at stage left across from JESUS, MARY and JOSEPH. After she is seated, the three kings enter, each with his gift.)*

KINGS *(enter slowly singing)*: "We three kings of orient are;
    bearing gifts we travel afar;
    Field and fountain; moor and mountain;
    following yonder star."[1]

KING ONE *(speaks or sings as he places his gift before MARY. These words could also be sung or spoken by soloist or group as each wise man offers his gift.)*: "Born a king on Bethlehem plain,
    gold I bring to crown him again;
    King forever, ceasing never,

---

[1] Words and music: John H. Hopkins, Jr., *Carols, Hymns & Songs*, 1863, based on Matthew 2:2-11.

over us all to reign."

(*KING ONE returns to his place with the other kings.*)

KING TWO: "Frankincense to offer have I,
  incense owns a deity nigh;
  Prayer and praising all men raising,
  worship him, God on high."

(*KING ONE returns to his place with the others.*)

KING THREE (*placing the perfume bottle before MARY*):
  "Myrrh is mine, its bitter perfume
  breathes a life of gathering gloom;
  Sorrowing, sighing, bleeding, dying,
  sealed in the stone-cold tomb."

(*KING THREE returns to his place with the others.*)

(*The OLDER MARY puts her arm around JESUS as if to protect
him after hearing this verse.*)

THE OLDER MARY: Oh, my son, I am often scared about the future.

JESUS: Mom, this life here on earth has joy and suffering for
  everyone. Life in heaven offers eternal joy for everybody who
  suffers here on earth.

JOSEPH: Jesus, there are so many times when I don't understand
  what you are talking about. But, you speak more wisdom than
  all the priests in the temple of Jerusalem. You are truly the son
  of God.

(*All, including YOUNG MARY, stand and sing or speak the final
verse of "We Three Kings."*)

ALL: "Glorious now behold him rise, king and God and sacrifice;
  Alleluia! Alleluia! sound through earth and skies."

(*The Holy Family members exit stage right. YOUNG MARY and
the three kings exit stage left.*)

2.
January 25: Feast of the Conversion of St. Paul or any of the Feasts of St. Paul

Cast of characters:
    ST. PAUL
    AARON and JORAM
    TWO TRADITIONAL JEWS
    VOICE OF JESUS (over public address system)
    ANANIAS, A CHRISTIAN

Props needed: None

> *(PAUL enters from stage right escorted by AARON and JORAM. They stop in the center of the stage.)*

AARON (*speaking as they enter*): Paul, do you think we were right in stoning Stephen?

PAUL: Yes! We *have* to make an example of these Christians who do not follow the laws of our religion and who believe this Jesus of Nazareth rose from the dead.

JORAM: I agree! This Christian, Stephen, had to be killed because the law says so for those who do not follow our sacred commandments.

PAUL: The high priest has asked me to go to Damascus to arrest Christians there and to bring them bound to Jerusalem.

JORAM: May you have good fortune, Paul. We shall look forward to your safe return.

AARON: Shalom, Paul. (*AARON and JORAM raise their hands in a farewell gesture as PAUL exits left.*)

PAUL: Shalom, Aaron. Shalom, Joram.

JORAM (*as he and AARON turn to exit right*): Paul is a remarkable man. He seems blessed by God.

AARON: You are right. Paul is remarkable. I sometimes wonder, however, if he doesn't persecute these Christians too fiercely.

JORAM: What do you mean? Those unbelievers like Stephen deserve to be persecuted and killed.

AARON: I suppose you are right, but I'm not sure Paul always believes in his heart that he should persecute those people who follow the teachings of the man called Jesus.

(*They exit right.*)

(*PAUL reenters slowly left. He is blind temporarily and extends his hands before him searching for objects that may be in his path.*)

PAUL: Lord, why do you rob me of my sight?

VOICE OF JESUS (*over public address system*): Paul, Paul, why are you persecuting me? (*PAUL falls to his knees.*) I am Jesus whom you persecute. Get up, go into Damascus and you will be told what you must do. [Acts 9:4-6]

(*PAUL begins a slow, awkward movement toward stage right as ANANIAS comes toward him with open arms.*)

ANANIAS (*as he touches PAUL*): Paul, my brother, the Lord Jesus, who appeared to you on the way here has sent me, Ananias, to help you recover your sight and be filled with the Holy Spirit. [Acts 9:17]

(*PAUL falls to his knees before ANANIAS who places his hands on PAUL's head.*)

PAUL: Oh, Lord Jesus, forgive me for torturing and killing those people who believe in you.

(*AARON and JORAM enter from right above ANANIAS and PAUL.*)

ANANIAS: May your sight be restored, Paul, and may you come to praise Jesus, our Lord and Savior, to all the peoples of Israel.

PAUL (*standing*): I can see again! Jesus, who says he is the Christ and the Son of God, has restored my sight. Praised be Jesus who is the savior of all the peoples of the earth!

AARON (*advancing toward PAUL*): Is this Paul who says these things?

JORAM (*following AARON*): It is truly Paul, who used to persecute Christians.

(*PAUL takes each by the arm and leads them to stage right.*)

PAUL: It is I, Paul, and I have seen a great light. The Christians have the true message of God. Jesus Christ is our Messiah who has risen from the dead. (*PAUL turns to wave to ANANIAS at left.*) Blessed be Jesus!

(*ANANIAS returns the gesture as all proclaim the final line.*)

ALL: Blessed be Jesus!

(*PAUL exits right with AARON and JORAM. ANANIAS exits left.*)

3.
January 31: Feast of St. John Bosco

Cast of characters:
  ST. JOHN BOSCO
  JOHN'S MOTHER
  ANTONIO, John's friend

Props needed: Cassock for John to wear

> (*JOHN enters the stage dressed in a cassock. His MOTHER walks beside him.*)

MOTHER: Oh, John, you look so nice in your cassock. I'm so proud of you.

JOHN: I didn't think the day I would enter the seminary would ever come.

MOTHER: You certainly wanted to learn about our Lord even in grade school. You know, at times it must have been hard for you to stay awake. You had to walk four miles to school every morning *after* you had done your work here at home first.

JOHN: Oh, it wasn't so far, Mother. I enjoyed seeing the animals in the fields and the birds in the sky.

MOTHER: You look handsome in that cassock, John, but remember clothes don't make the man. You must be worthy of your vocation. If at any time you feel unsure of your calling, please come home. I would rather have you do something else than be an unworthy priest.

JOHN: You have my word, Mother. I won't continue studying for the priesthood if I have any doubts.

> (*ANTONIO enters.*)

ANTONIO: John, where did you get that outfit?

JOHN: We must wear this in the seminary. It's called a cassock.

ANTONIO: Well, it looks like a dress to me. (*He mimics a lady swaying her skirts and then says mockingly*) You'll look very cute when you parade down the aisle of our parish church.

JOHN (*catches ANTONIO from behind and puts an armlock on him*): Tony, you better watch it. I can still out-wrestle you—cassock or not.

ANTONIO: Ouch, John! That hurts! Let me go!

MOTHER (*coming up behind JOHN*): John, let Antonio go!

JOHN: All right, Antonio. Will you promise to pray hard for me that I will be a good priest?

ANTONIO: Yes! Yes! Just let me go.

(*JOHN lets ANTONIO loose.*)

JOHN: Don't forget to pray!

ANTONIO: I'm going to pray for all those sinners you're going to wrestle for God.

JOHN: I'm not interested in wrestling. I want to start schools for young boys and girls so that they can learn a trade or a craft and can also learn about Jesus Christ. It's important that young people learn how Christ is present in everything we do—in our work, in our play, in our studies.

MOTHER: To do that, you'll need lots of energy. Come on, you two, (*they all start to leave the stage*) I have a wonderful spaghetti dinner for John's last night at home.

(*exiting*)

JOHN: I hope it's spaghetti with sausage.

ANTONIO: I like ravioli!

MOTHER: What would you say to some of both? (*They are off stage.*)

4.
February 2: Feast of the Presentation of the Lord

Cast of characters:
> NARRATOR
> MARY
> JOSEPH
> SIMEON
> ANNA

Props needed: Baby doll to represent Jesus
> Box of doves (these can be toys)

Music: "Joy to the World"

> (*The NARRATOR comes to the microphone. MARY and JOSEPH should be ready to enter immediately following; MARY holds the baby doll and JOSEPH holds a small box or bird cage with two mock doves inside.*)

NARRATOR: When the day came to purify them according to the law of Moses (*MARY and JOSEPH enter slowly from stage right to the center of the acting space*), they took him up to Jerusalem to present him to the Lord, just as it is written in the law of the Lord, "Every firstborn male shall be blessed for the Lord's service." [Luke 2:22-23]

MARY (*turns to JOSEPH*): Joseph, are the turtledoves all right?

JOSEPH: They are fine, MARY. The Lord will be pleased with our gift in honor of our son.

NARRATOR: There lived in Jerusalem at the time a certain man named Simeon. He was just and pious (*SIMEON enters from stage left to halfway to MARY and JOSEPH*) and waited for the savior of Israel, and the Holy Spirit was upon him. [Luke 2:25]

SIMEON: Good people, it has been revealed to me by the Holy Spirit that I shall not die until I have seen the Savior of the world. [Luke 2:26]

JOSEPH: We have brought our firstborn boy, Jesus, to be blessed for the service of the Lord. (*MARY gives the baby to SIMEON.*)

SIMEON: May the Lord bless this child, Jesus. Lord, you can dismiss your servant Simeon in peace; you have carried out your word. For my eyes have seen your saving deed displayed for all the peoples to see; a revealing light to the Gentiles, glory for your people Israel. May God's blessing be upon you, Mary and Joseph. [Luke 2:28-32]

(*ANNA has entered to the left of SIMEON from stage left.*)

MARY: Thank you, Simeon, for your blessing.

SIMEON (*returning the baby to MARY*): This child will bring about the rise and fall of many people in Israel. He will meet many people who don't like him or his ways and you yourself shall suffer so that others can be saved. [Luke 2:34-35]

ANNA: Simeon, this is the person the prophets have spoken about. What a beautiful child! What is his name?

JOSEPH: His name is Jesus!

ANNA: Jesus! His name means, "The Lord is salvation"! He is the Messiah—our Holy One, who will save the people.

MARY: I shall treasure these things in my heart.

JOSEPH (*hands doves' box or cage to SIMEON*): Simeon, this is our offering to the Lord for the blessing of our son, Jesus.

SIMEON: Thank you, Joseph. May you, Mary and your son grow in the grace of God.

(*As MARY and JOSEPH exit right and SIMEON exits left, the choir or congregation sings "Joy to the World."*)

5.
February 3: Feast of St. Blase

Cast of characters:
    ST. BLASE
    SOLDIER ONE
    SOLDIER TWO
    A WOMAN
    CHILD, of preschool or primary age

Props needed: None

> (*ST. BLASE enters wearing a bishop's garb or prisoner's rags. He is shoved from stage right into acting area by two Roman SOLDIERS.*)

SOLDIER ONE: Move on, you Christian dreamer!

SOLDIER TWO: They call this Blase their bishop.

SOLDIER ONE: That means he's the Christian leader here.

SOLDIER TWO: He'll regret he has that title when we chop off his head.

BLASE (*turning to them from center*): I'll regret nothing! No sacrifice is too great when it's done in the name of the Lord. Besides, I shall see the Lord sooner if I am killed this way.

> (*A WOMAN enters stage left with a small CHILD.*)

SOLDIER ONE (*"striking" BLASE*): Be quiet, Christian! You'll have your chance to speak before Agricolus, the governor of Armenia.

WOMAN (*crossing with the CHILD to the left of BLASE at stage center*): Oh, beloved Bishop Blase, please cure my child who has a terrible sore throat.

BLASE: I can't cure anyone. If your child is cured, it's because of your faith in our Lord Jesus Christ.

WOMAN: Please help my child!

BLASE (*to soldiers*): Is it all right if I help her?

SOLDIER ONE: Go ahead. Nothing will happen, I'm sure.

> (*BLASE puts his hands on the CHILD's throat.*)

BLASE: May God deliver you from diseases of the throat and from every other evil. (*blessing the CHILD*) In the name of the Father and of the Son and of the Holy Spirit. Amen.

WOMAN: Oh, thank you Bishop! I know God will hear your prayer.

> (*SOLDIERS shove BLASE past the WOMAN and CHILD toward stage left.*)

SOLDIER TWO: Now, Christian, Agricolus is waiting to sentence you.

SOLDIER ONE: Blase can say good-bye to this Christian mumbo-jumbo.

CHILD: Mommy, my throat doesn't hurt anymore. It feels better!

WOMAN: Come, child, we must hurry home and tell your father what has happened. Praise be to our good Bishop Blase!

BLASE (*turns with SOLDIERS before exiting*): No, good woman, praise be to our God who cured your child!

> (*WOMAN and CHILD exit stage right; BLASE and the SOLDIERS exit stage left.*)

6.
February 14: St. Valentine's Day

Although St. Valentine is no longer in the official roll of the saints, he represents a spirit of sacrificial love. Since our society still likes to celebrate St. Valentine's Day, this play could help emphasize Valentine's spirit of love.

Cast of characters:
> ST. VALENTINE
> ST. STEPHEN
> ST. AGATHA
> ST. LAWRENCE
> ST. MARIA GORETTI

Props needed: Valentines for each saint

Music: "I Have Loved You" or another song about Christian love

> (*VALENTINE, dressed in the red of martyrs, enters from stage right to center.*)

VALENTINE: Greetings, everyone. Many people today think that I am not real. They like the wonderful story of my life. But, really, I am much more than a story. I am also the person who helps the Christian martyrs, such as.... (*As VALENTINE says each of the following names, the martyrs enter alternately stage right and stage left.*)

> (*ST. STEPHEN enters stage right and crosses to stage center.*)

St. Stephen was the first martyr. He was a deacon stoned to death two years after the Lord's Resurrection.

> (*ST. AGATHA enters stage left and crosses to stage center.*)

St. Agatha was martyred and entered heaven after being persecuted by the Roman senator Quintanius.

> (*ST. LAWRENCE enters stage right and stands to the right

of ST. STEPHEN.)

St. Lawrence helped the poor people of Rome until the emperor Valerian ordered St. Lawrence killed.

(*ST. MARIA GORETTI enters stage left and stands to the left of ST. AGATHA.*)

St. Maria Goretti was a young teenager who was killed when she fought back against someone who tried to hurt her. (*slight pause*) All these martyrs loved Jesus very much and they died trying to live like him.

VALENTINE (*continuing*): Now I will show you the way which is better than all others.

AGATHA: If I speak in human and angelic tongues, but do not have love, I am a noisy gong or a clanging cymbal. [1 Corinthians 13:1]

LAWRENCE: And if I have the gift of prophecy and understand all knowledge, comprehend all mysteries, [13:2]

STEPHEN: if I have faith enough to move mountains, but have not love, I am nothing.

MARIA: If I give everything I have to feed the poor and hand over my body, but I do not have love, I gain nothing. [13:3]

AGATHA and MARIA: Love is patient; love is kind. Love is not jealous, it does not put on airs, it is not snobbish. [13:4]

VALENTINE, STEPHEN and LAWRENCE: Love is not rude, it is not self-seeking, it is not quick to anger; neither does it brood over injuries. Love does not rejoice in what is wrong but rejoices with the truth. [13:5-6]

ALL: There is no limit to love's patience, to its trust, its hope, its power to endure. [13:7]

VALENTINE (*to others*): I have a card for each of you. It will be a love letter like the ones we Romans used to send in honor of the pagan goddess, Februata Juno.

(*VALENTINE hands each of the martyrs on stage a card from*

which each saint reads. VALENTINE announces the saint's name as he hands each card to that martyr.)

VALENTINE: Maria.

MARIA (*reading the note*): Love never fails, prophecies will cease, tongues will be silent, knowledge will pass away. [13:8]

VALENTINE (*handing him a card*): Lawrence.

LAWRENCE (*reading from the card*): Our knowledge is imperfect and our prophesying is imperfect. When the perfect comes, the imperfect will pass away. [13:9-10]

VALENTINE (*handing her a card*): Agatha.

AGATHA (*reading from the card*): When I was a child, I used to talk like a child, think like a child, reason like a child. [13:11]

STEPHEN (*reading the note*): When I became a man, I put childish ways aside. Now we see indistinctly, as if looking in a mirror; then we shall see face to face. [13:11-12]

VALENTINE: My knowledge is imperfect now; then I shall know even as I am known. [13:12]

ALL: There are in the end three things that last: faith, hope and love, and the greatest of these is love. [13:13]

(All sing chorus of "I Have Loved You" or other song about Christian love.)

(At the end of the song, STEPHEN, LAWRENCE and VALENTINE exit stage right while MARIA and AGATHA exit stage left.)

7.
March 17: Feast of St. Patrick

Cast of characters:
> Three younger children: SEAN, MARY and JAMES
> BRIDGIT, an older child

Props needed: Four three-leaf clovers—can be made of green construction paper. You may want to make enough paper clovers for each child in the congregation.

Music needed: "Song of St. Patrick"

> *(Three "Irish" children, all clad in clothing including something green, enter stage left looking for four-leaf clovers. They are SEAN [pronounced "Shawn"], MARY and JAMES.)*

SEAN: Have you spotted any four-leaf clovers yet, Mary?

MARY: No, Sean, I haven't. I think these are all three-leaf clovers.

JAMES: I think so, too. Why don't we just give up?

SEAN: No! Today's the feast day of St. Patrick. Surely we'll have good luck today and find a four-leaf clover.

> *(BRIDGIT enters from stage right.)*

BRIDGIT: Hello.

MARY: Happy St. Patrick's Day, Bridgit!

BRIDGIT: That's right! It's the feast day of our country's patron.

JAMES: What's a patron?

BRIDGIT (*drawing JAMES closer to her as she answers his question*): A patron is like a father or mother, someone who looks after you. St. Patrick is very close to God and we can ask St. Patrick to ask the Lord for some favor we need.

SEAN: That sounds like my older brother, Frank. I sometimes ask him to mention to Dad about something I'd like to have. He seems to know what to say to Dad better than I do.

BRIDGIT: That's a good way to look at a patron saint, Sean. A patron saint knows God so well that he or she can use the right words in asking God for what we need.

MARY: I like having St. Patrick for our patron.

JAMES: Why? What was he like?

SEAN: Well, he came from either Scotland or England. One day when he was walking along the shore, he and a bunch of other teenagers were grabbed by pirates who then sailed to Ireland. In Ireland all of the teenagers were sold as slaves. Patrick was bought by a chieftain who needed a shepherd for his herd of sheep and swine.

JAMES: That's right. Patrick became a sheepherder.

MARY: I bet he had lots of baked ham and lamb chops!

BRIDGIT: I don't think his masters were very kind to him. He escaped from Ireland and went to a monastery in France where he studied to be a priest.

MARY: What happened to him then?

SEAN: He was made a bishop. He knew that God wanted him to return to Ireland to teach the Irish people about Jesus Christ. So Patrick and his helpers, called missionaries, went back to Ireland.

MARY: Patrick walked all over Ireland, telling people about Jesus and how they should try to live like Jesus. Patrick baptized thousands of people, helped build hundreds of churches, and ordained many priests and bishops. In thirty years all of Ireland became Christian—thanks to Patrick!

JAMES: Why is March 17 so special to St. Patrick?

BRIDGIT: It's the day he died in the monastery of St. Paul in Ulster.

SEAN (*surprised*): We celebrate the day he died?

JAMES (*giving SEAN a slight shove*): Of course! The day he died is his birthday into heaven. (*SEAN turns away and starts looking for four-leaf clovers again.*)

BRIDGIT: That's true, of course, for all the saints. The greatest day of their lives, just like it is for all of us, is the day when we meet Jesus face to face. (*noticing SEAN*) What are you looking for, Sean?

SEAN: We've all been looking for four-leaf clovers.

MARY: They're a sign of good luck, you know.

BRIDGIT: St. Patrick would have preferred the three-leaf clover. (*She shows the others one of four three-leaf clovers she has already picked.*) He believed that our three-leaf clover, which is so easily found, represents God the Father, the Son and the Holy Spirit.

JAMES: I never thought of it like that before, but each leaf is like one of the persons in the Holy Trinity.

MARY: So, Sean, we can stop searching for four-leaf clovers since the three-leaf clovers are signs from God.

BRIDGIT: Here is a clover for each of you that I picked today.

(*If the school or parish wishes to provide three-leaf clovers cut out of green construction paper with "Father," "Son" and "Holy Spirit" printed individually on each leaf, these can be distributed now. BRIDGIT would add: "In fact I have one for everyone here if you'll help me distribute them, MARY, SEAN, JAMES and [adds the names of any other helpers]. As everyone receives a clover, let's sing a hymn to St. Patrick." After singing "Song of St. Patrick" or after BRIDGIT's "that I picked today" above:*)

MARY: I'll always remember St. Patrick as the one who told everybody in Ireland about Jesus and the Holy Trinity.

JAMES: Every time we pick a clover we can remember God the Father, the Son and the Holy Spirit.

BRIDGIT: We should be off to school.

SEAN (*looking around him, as everyone moves off the stage*): These three-leaf clovers are everywhere.

BRIDGIT: Maybe it's because the good Lord is everywhere.

(*They exit.*)

8.
March 19: Feast of St. Joseph

(Note: Encourage children/actors to improvise with words.)

Cast of characters:
    JOSEPH
    MARY
    JESUS as a twelve-year-old

Props needed: Two fitted boards (one is grooved so the other board
    fits into it)
    Two matching boards

Music needed: A prayer to St. Joseph

    *(JOSEPH enters from stage right with two fitted boards. JOSEPH
    is fitting the boards together as he works on a carpentry project.
    MARY enters from stage right and crosses to JOSEPH at stage
    center.)*

MARY: Joseph, are you nearly finished with the cupboard?

JOSEPH: Well, Mary, I have two more pieces to fit together and then
    it will be ready for the Levi family.

    (JESUS arrives from stage left with two more boards.)

JESUS: Dad, are these the boards you wanted?

JOSEPH: Yes, Jesus. Can you cut a groove of three inches by
    one-half inch in one of them?

JESUS: Sure, Dad.

MARY: Joseph, you're not going to charge the Levis for the
    cupboard, are you? Ben Levi has been ill and hasn't worked for
    weeks.

JOSEPH: I didn't know that, Mary. That means they'll have no food
    to put in the cupboard.

JESUS: Why don't we let other people know the Levis need food and clothing?

MARY: That's a very good idea, Jesus.

JESUS: I'll visit each family in our neighborhood to see if they can share with the Levis.

JOSEPH: Why don't I make another cupboard with the lumber left over from the Levis's cupboard? Then we can sell the second cupboard to raise money to help the Levis.

JESUS (*exiting stage left*): I'll run to tell everyone about the Levis and how they can use our help. (*Exits.*)

JOSEPH: Mary, we have a wonderful son!

MARY: And you're wonderful, too! Jesus is a lot like you. He's always thinking of other people, especially people like the Levis who need our help. You're really a good father to him, Joseph, and a good example, too.

(They exit stage right as the choir or congregation recites a prayer to St. Joseph.)

9.
March 25: Feast of the Annunciation of the Lord

Cast of characters:
> FOUR CHILDREN (dressed in white)
> ANGEL
> MARY (dressed in blue and white)

Props needed: None

Music: Marian hymn such as "Immaculate Mary," "Hail, Holy Queen Enthroned Above," "Hail Mary: Gentle Woman," "My Soul Rejoices," "Sing of Mary," "Be Joyful, Mary," "Blessed Mary/ Ave Maria," "Mary, Full of Grace" or other hymn.

> *(The FOUR CHILDREN enter from stage left and remain standing from left to center while MARY enters from stage right and, when she is halfway to stage center, kneels.)*

CHILDREN: A flower has sprung *(gesture with right hands to the ground)* from Jesse's stock and a star has risen *(gesture with left hands up, as if to heaven)* from Jacob.

> *(The ANGEL has entered from stage right and stands behind MARY during the previous speech.)*

CHILDREN: The Virgin will give birth to a savior. *(Both hands of each CHILD go up, as if toward heaven.)*

ANGEL: Blessed are you, O Virgin Mary, for you will become the mother of the Most High.

MARY: How can this be since I do not know man?

ANGEL: The Holy Spirit will come to you, Mary, and the power of the Most High will be over you. [Luke 1:35]

MARY: My soul proclaims the Lord's greatness, my spirit finds joy in

God my savior, who has looked upon this servant in her lowliness. [Luke 1:46-48] (*The ANGEL exits stage right. MARY stands and turns forward.*)

CHILDREN (*arms extended toward MARY*): All ages to come shall call you blessed. God who is mighty has done great things for you. Holy is God's name.

(*The choir sings a Marian hymn and all CHILDREN including the one playing MARY turn toward the statue of MARY while the hymn is sung. Afterwards, MARY exits stage right and the other CHILDREN exit stage left.*)

10.
April 25: Feast of St. Mark

Cast of characters:
    MARK
    THREE GIRLS
    PAUL
    PETER

Props needed: None

Music needed: "Jesus Christ Is Risen Today"

> *(Three boys enter from stage right and three girls enter from stage left. All cross to stage center where they form a semicircle.)*

ALL: The Lord will give his message to the preachers of the gospel.

> *(They chant an "alleluia" which the congregation repeats.)*

> *(MARK steps forward.)*

MARK: My name is Mark. I'm the cousin of Barnabas and I wrote one of the four Gospels.

ALL: Come, let us worship the Lord who speaks to us through the gospel, alleluia.

MARK: I traveled with St. Paul on his first missionary journey and later I went with him to Rome.

ALL: The Lord will give him strength to proclaim it fearlessly, alleluia.

> *(PAUL steps forward from the group during the preceding verse.)*

PAUL: Mark, I love you like a brother. In your Gospel, you wrote down the stories about Jesus that you heard from our leader, Peter.

> *(PETER steps forward as MARK speaks.)*

MARK: Paul, you and Peter are the great leaders of our Church after the death of Jesus.

PETER: I spoke to our Jewish brothers and sisters and explained to them how Jesus Christ is the Messiah.

PAUL: I spoke to the Gentiles of Rome, Greece and Asia about the teachings and actions of Jesus and how he rose from the dead.

(PETER and PAUL step back into the group.)

ALL: For it is Jesus who chose apostles, prophets, pastors and teachers to build up the body of Christ.

MARK: Jesus Christ has truly risen from the dead and our Gospels proclaim the good news.

(MARK steps back into the group as all sing a setting of "Jesus Christ Is Risen Today." Afterwards, the boys exit stage right and the girls exit stage left.)

11.
June 24: Feast of St. John the Baptist

Cast of characters:
    ST. JOHN THE BAPTIST (as an adult)
    TWO GIRL DISCIPLES
    TWO BOY DISCIPLES

Props needed: None

    (*ST. JOHN THE BAPTIST enters stage right dressed in a short tunic. He is followed by TWO GIRL DISCIPLES while TWO BOY DISCIPLES enter from stage left and stand at the left of JOHN as he moves to stage center.*)

ST. JOHN THE BAPTIST (*speaking as he enters*): Prepare the way of the Lord! He is coming and I am not worthy to tie his sandal. [Luke 3:4-17]

GIRL ONE: Who are you talking about, John?

ST. JOHN THE BAPTIST: He is the Lord, the Messiah. He is the one whom the prophets of old had predicted would come to save sinners.

BOY TWO: How will we know him, John?

ST. JOHN THE BAPTIST: You will know him by his works. He will make the lame walk, the deaf hear, and the blind see. [Isaiah 35:5]

GIRL TWO: Shall we follow him, John, and not you?

ST. JOHN THE BAPTIST: Yes, I am only a messenger. I go before the Lord to prepare his way.

BOY ONE: John, take us to him.

ST. JOHN THE BAPTIST: The Lord's time has not come; but, follow me (*ST. JOHN THE BAPTIST crosses to stage left and the others follow*) and we will see what good we can do now. We can spread the good news that the Messiah is coming.

ALL (*speaking as they exit stage left*): Prepare the way of the Lord!
Prepare the way of the Lord!

12.
July 11: Feast of St. Benedict

Cast of characters:
    BENEDICT, a young man
    ROMANUS, his teacher

Props needed: None

Music: Hymn to St. Benedict or written by a Benedictine composer,
    perhaps "A Hymn of Glory Let Us Sing"

(*BENEDICT and ROMANUS enter from stage left and move to
stage center. ROMANUS leads.*)

ROMANUS (*speaking as they enter*): Must you leave, Benedict?

BENEDICT: Yes, Master Romanus. You have taught me much about
    loving the Lord here in Subiaco. I have shared this knowledge
    with my community of men.

ROMANUS: May God bless you in all your endeavors, Benedict.

BENEDICT: The rule I will develop for the brothers will be one of
    love. The rule will guide people on how to pray, how to study,
    how to work and how to live together peacefully. The monks
    will try to outdo one another in love. They will love the Lord,
    one another and all people who visit our house. The monks
    should not follow what they think is good for themselves. They
    should always think of others first. [Rule of St. Benedict]

ROMANUS: Blessed be the Lord. And you and your brothers will be
    blessed for helping others.

BENEDICT (*moving toward stage right*): Come, Master Romanus.
    Let's tell the brothers about my move to Monte Cassino. I want
    monks from many places to gather here to live and pray
    together. We must prepare for the journey.

ROMANUS (*following BENEDICT*): I will tell your parents and your sister, Scholastica, about your new home. We will visit you in a few weeks.

BENEDICT (*as they exit stage right*): We'll look forward to seeing you. All people will always be welcome in our home. We shall call our home an abbey. Be sure to visit us!

(The choir and congregation can sing a hymn to St. Benedict or one written by a Benedictine [O.S.B.].)

13.
July 31: Feast of St. Ignatius of Loyola;
December 3: Feast of St. Francis Xavier

Cast of characters:
> ST. IGNATIUS
> ST. FRANCIS XAVIER
> SIX JESUITS

Props needed: Writing paper, two pens, two desks, two chairs

Music or recitation: "Take Lord, Receive" by St. Ignatius

> (*ST. IGNATIUS and ST. FRANCIS XAVIER enter from stage right and left, respectively, and cross halfway to stage center. They speak as if reciting letters.*)

ST. FRANCIS XAVIER: Dear Superior General Ignatius, India is a wonderful land. There are many villages where people became Christians years ago. But now there are no priests here to say Mass for the people and give them the sacraments.

ST. IGNATIUS: Dear Francis Xavier, I am happy to hear that you are teaching the children to say the Apostles' Creed, the Our Father and Hail Mary. It is sad that these people of India have no priests or religious today.

ST. FRANCIS XAVIER: Dear Ignatius, if I could, I would go to all the universities of Europe and tell people that we need missionaries in India. People in India might never know Jesus Christ if there are no priests and religious.

> (*The SIX JESUITS enter; three join IGNATIUS at stage right and three join FRANCIS XAVIER at stage left.*)

ST. IGNATIUS: Dear Francis Xavier, greetings! Our group of priests who are called Jesuits is growing. Soon we will have many new priests and others to help you in India. God bless you, Francis

Xavier, and the Jesuits as you go to missions to tell people about Jesus.

ALL (*recite or sing John Foley, S.J.'s setting of this prayer from* Spiritual Exercises, *no. 234*):

Take Lord, receive (*hands upward, palms upward*)
All my liberty (*hands upward and outward from body*)
my memory, (*right hand on forehead*)
understanding,
my entire will. (*hands crossed over chests*)
Give me only your love (*right hands to hearts*)
and your grace (*make sign of cross*)
your love and your grace (*hands upward and outward*)
are enough for me. (*hands together as if in prayer*)
Take Lord, (*hands upward, palms upward*)
receive, (*hands higher, palms upward*)
all I have and possess. (*hands wider, as if offering possessions*)
You have given all to me; (*arms across chests*)
now I return it. (*hands outward and upward*)

(*Repeat from the first "Take Lord" through "my entire will."*)

(*The four on the right exit stage right and the four on the left exit stage left.*)

14.
August 1: Feast of St. Alphonsus Liguori

Cast of characters:
  ST. ALPHONSUS LIGUORI
  TWO REDEMPTORISTS
  MARIA, a child

Props needed: A lollipop for ST. ALPHONSUS to give MARIA

  (*ST. ALPHONSUS enters stage right with TWO REDEMPTORISTS following him. They cross to stage center.*)

ST. ALPHONSUS: My friends, I resigned my position as bishop. I would rather be with you and work among the poor.

REDEMPTORIST ONE: Father Alphonsus, we are glad to have you with us.

REDEMPTORIST TWO: Father Alphonsus, why did you call our order the Redemptorists, the Order of the Redeemer?

ST. ALPHONSUS: Jesus Christ is the holiest and most perfect of persons. He will redeem us and take us to heaven if we follow his ways.

REDEMPTORIST ONE: It is our job as Redemptorists to continue Christ's work of saving people here on earth.

REDEMPTORIST TWO: Some people seem to work against their own salvation.

ST. ALPHONSUS: The Lord gave us every good thing we need to be saved: grace, love and heaven. His mercy is open to all, even to those who seem to be careless in receiving God's love and mercy.

  (*MARIA runs on stage from left and hugs ST. ALPHONSUS.*)

MARIA: Father Alphonsus, Father Alphonsus! I'm so glad you are here!

ST. ALPHONSUS: Maria, I am happy to see you.

MARIA: Father, do you have something for me?

ST. ALPHONSUS: I have God's love for you. (*He gives MARIA another hug.*)

MARIA: Oh, Father Alphonsus, you know what I mean. I know about God's love and how I shall always have it.

ST. ALPHONSUS (*pulling out a lollipop, which he holds up*): Is this what you mean, Maria?

MARIA: Oh, Father Alphonsus, you remembered! (*ALPHONSUS gives MARIA the candy.*) I'm so happy!

ST. ALPHONSUS: God's love is sweeter than that candy, Maria.

MARIA: Father Alphonsus, come with me to the garden. (*They move stage left and appear to be admiring a garden of flowers.*) The flowers are also proof of God's love.

ST. ALPHONSUS: Everything in creation, Maria, is part of God's gift to us. (*They exit stage left, and the two REDEMPTORISTS exit stage right.*)

15.
August 6: Feast of the Transfiguration of the Lord

Cast of characters:
>   JESUS
>   PETER
>   JAMES
>   JOHN
>   MOSES
>   ELIJAH
>   VOICE OF GOD

Props needed: None

> (*JESUS enters from stage right with PETER following him. JAMES and JOHN enter at a faster pace from stage left. They all meet at stage center.*)

JAMES (*panting*): I thought we lost you on the mountain.

JOHN: I wasn't worried. I told James that Jesus would find us.

PETER: Why are we here, Jesus?

JESUS: I wanted you to meet my friends, Moses and Elijah. (*JESUS moves left beyond JAMES and JOHN. MOSES and ELIJAH enter quietly from stage left.*) They are very special to all of us.

JAMES and JOHN (*almost falling back against PETER as they exclaim in awe*): Moses...Elijah!

JESUS: Did God say that I must die so that people can be saved?

MOSES: Yes, Jesus. But you shall rise from the dead on the third day after your death.

ELIJAH: We are looking forward to your joining us once again in heaven.

MOSES and ELIJAH (*speaking simultaneously*): Shalom, Messiah, Shalom. (*They exit slowly stage left.*)

PETER (*JESUS turns to the right to listen to him.*): Lord, how good that we are here! With your permission I will erect three booths here: one for you, one for Moses and one for Elijah. [Matthew 17:4]

GOD (*speaking over the public address system*): This is my Beloved Son on whom my favor rests. Listen to him. [Matthew 17:5] (*The three apostles fall to the floor.*)

JESUS (*after a pause*): Get up! Don't be afraid. [Matthew 17:7] (*JESUS crosses to stage center.*)

(*The three apostles stand up and smooth their garments.*)

JESUS: Do not tell anyone of this vision until the Son of Man rises from the dead. [Matthew 17:9]

PETER: Lord, why do the scribes claim that Elijah must come first? [Matthew 17:10]

JESUS: Elijah has already come. But they did not recognize him and they did as they pleased with him. [Matthew 17:12]

JOHN: You are speaking of John the Baptist.

JESUS (*crossing before them to stage right*): The Son of Man will suffer at their hands in the same way.

JAMES: Jesus, don't say this.

JESUS: Unless I die, you and others cannot rise from sin into eternal life as I shall do the third day after my death. Come, let's go to the people. (*JESUS exits stage right and the others follow.*)

16.
September 14: Feast of the Triumph of the Cross

Cast of characters:
    TWO BOYS
    THREE GIRLS

Props needed: None

Music: "Lift High the Cross," "Take Up Your Cross," "When I Survey the Wondrous Cross," "Wood of the Cross," "Were You There?" or another hymn about the cross

> *(TWO BOYS enter from stage left and THREE GIRLS enter from stage right. They are wearing surplices or choir robes. Let the THREE GIRLS and TWO BOYS form the horizontal and vertical beams of the cross.)*

ALL: We are celebrating the feast of the cross which drove away darkness (*right arms, palms outward gesture as if pushing the darkness away*) and brought in the light (*left arms, palms upward gesture, as if bringing the light forward*). [Speech by St. Andrew of Crete, bishop]

BOY ONE: As we keep this feast, we are lifted up (*all raise both arms, palms upward and outward*) with the crucified Christ, leaving behind us earth and sin so that we may gain the things above.

GIRL ONE: So great and outstanding a possession is the cross that the one who wins it has won a treasure.

ALL: The cross is something wonderfully great and honorable.

GIRL ONE: The cross is great because Christ achieved his greatest triumph through the cross.

> *(All make the sign of the cross in the air before them with their right hands.)*

ALL: The cross is something wonderfully great and honorable.

GIRL THREE: The cross is honorable because it is both the sign of God's suffering and the trophy of his victory. (*All extend both hands high as if lifting up a crown.*)

ALL: The cross is something wonderfully great and honorable.

BOY TWO: Now you can see that the cross is Christ's glory and triumph. (*All bring their hands down into a praying position with both palms together.*)

ALL: The cross is something wonderfully great and honorable.

(*The people form the cross in place while the choir and/or congregation sing "Lift High the Cross," "Take Up Your Cross," "When I Survey the Wondrous Cross," "Wood of the Cross," "Were You There?" or some other hymn about the cross. When the song is finished, the THREE GIRLS exit stage right and the TWO BOYS exit stage left.*)

17.
October 4: Feast of St. Francis of Assisi

Cast of characters
> ST. FRANCIS OF ASSISI
> FOUR FRANCISCAN FRIARS

Props needed: None

Music: "Prayer of St. Francis"

> (*FRANCIS should be between two of his FRIARS as they walk from stage right to stage center. Two other FRIARS come from stage left. The actors should be dressed in the brown robes of the Franciscans or in some neutral clothing of dark shirts and trousers. FRANCIS is dying and should be assisted by the two FRIARS on either side of him.*)

FRANCIS (*once at stage center*): People have always called me "little poor man."

FRIAR ONE: That's because you gave up everything you owned— your shoes, your clothes, your money. You wanted to live like the poor people you served. You lived the way Jesus told us in the Gospel.

FRIAR TWO: You love nature. You always say we should love everything God created—mice and cats and wolves and flowers and sunshine and wind and rocks and fire.

FRANCIS: The birds are my favorite. Sometimes they make so much noise when I preach. I have to tell them to be quiet so everyone can hear the words of God.

FRIAR THREE: You have blessed the birds of the earth and sky and called each animal your "sister" and "brother."

FRIAR FOUR: You, more than the rest of us, have cared for the sick and poor. You have showed us how we should help others.

(The two FRIARS who have been supporting FRANCIS lay him down.)

FRANCIS: The songs of the birds are so sweet! When I no longer hear those songs, I know I will be in heaven.

(The FRIARS gather around FRANCIS.)

FRANCIS: Bring my soul out of prison, Lord, so that I may give thanks to your name. The just will gather around me when you have been good to me. [Adaptation of Psalm 142:8]

(FRANCIS places his arms diagonally across his chest and lowers his head slowly to suggest death.)

ALL FRIARS: Blessed is Francis. His name will always stand for love and kindness to all people and creatures.

(They remain still or join in singing "Prayer of St. Francis." After the song, the five actors exit in the same direction from which they came.)

18.
October 15: Feast of St. Teresa of Avila;
December 14: Feast of St. John of the Cross

Cast of characters:
    ST. TERESA OF AVILA
    ST. JOHN OF THE CROSS

Props needed: None

Music: Chant of "Gloria Patri"

> *(ST. TERESA and ST. JOHN OF THE CROSS enter from stage left and cross to stage center. TERESA enters first while JOHN is speaking.)*

ST. JOHN: Oh, Teresa. You have just been through a sad time. I know you have prayed a lot and been alone often. Sometimes it is good for us to experience these things. It can bring us closer to God.

ST. TERESA: John, I know this is true. I really didn't know how much I love Jesus until I felt separated from him.

ST. JOHN: But you know now, don't you, that you will never be really separated from Jesus. We may give up on the Lord, but the Lord will never give up on us.

ST. TERESA: John, my heart belongs to God. I pray so often to God and I know that God wants me to help other people pray. I try to live my life for others—through my prayers and my actions. I tell our Carmelite sisters and friars that they should pray, too, and be good examples to other people.

ST. JOHN: Teresa, we shall always be brother and sister.

ST. TERESA: That's true, John. But we must remember that all women and men are our sisters and brothers.

> *(JOHN and TERESA exit stage left.)*

19.
October 18: Feast of St. Luke

Cast of characters:
    ST. LUKE
    ST. PAUL

Music: "How Firm a Foundation"

> *(ST. PAUL enters from stage left to stage center while ST. LUKE enters slightly after ST. PAUL from stage right and hurries to meet him at stage center.)*

ST. LUKE: Paul, I'm so glad I found you.

ST. PAUL: What's upsetting you, Luke?

ST. LUKE: The Roman government has issued orders to arrest you.

ST. PAUL (*sarcastically*): At least as a Roman citizen, I shall have the "privilege" of being beheaded.

ST. LUKE: Peter also has been accused of being a traitor to the Roman government. The Romans are trying to get rid of our leaders because we are Christians.

ST. PAUL: You are a doctor and well-educated, Luke. You must write the story of our Lord's life here on earth. In your stories you must tell people that God said his Church will last forever.

ST. LUKE: I'll do that, Paul. I'll dedicate my life to telling the Good News about Jesus Christ. I'll talk to people who knew Jesus. Then I'll write about Jesus and what he did.

ST. PAUL: Remember, Luke. Tell everyone to be of strong faith! Jesus is with us always!

ST. LUKE: I will, Paul! I'll tell our story so everyone will know Jesus Christ!

> *(LUKE and PAUL exit stage left.)*

20.
November 1: Feast of All Saints

Cast of characters:
SEVEN ACTORS, including one representing ST. JOHN, dressed in albs or choir robes

Props needed: None

Music: "For All the Saints"

(*SEVEN ACTORS enter from stage right to stage left and form either a semicircle or a V-shape. ST. JOHN's part is spoken by the fourth actor from the right.*)

ALL (*sung or spoken once the arrangement has been formed*):

For all the saints who from their labors rest,
Who thee by faith before the world confessed,
Thy name, O Jesus, be forever blest. Alleluia, alleluia![2]

ST. JOHN: Let's have a roll call of the saints.

SPEAKER ONE: (*from the right*) Anthony, Anna, Bernard, Clare,

SPEAKER TWO: Basil, Agnes, Angela, Stephen,

SPEAKER THREE: Rose, Francis, Augustine, Maria,

SPEAKER FOUR: Elizabeth Seton, Thomas, Patrick, Mary Magdalene,

SPEAKER FIVE: Bridget, James, Catherine, John,

SPEAKER SIX: Louis, Veronica, Teresa, Michael,

SPEAKER SEVEN: Gregory, Monica, Lawrence, Martha.

ST. JOHN: There are saints who prophesy (*extends right arm forward, palm downward*) and help us understand the will of God.

[2]William W. Howe, 1823-1897, *For All the Saints*.

SPEAKER TWO: There are saints who praise the Lord in word (*gestures to lips*) and song (*extends gesture forward*).

SPEAKER THREE: There are saints who help the poor and suffering (*wipes someone's brow or feeds someone*).

SPEAKER FOUR: There are saints who teach (*holds a make-believe book*) others about Jesus.

SPEAKER FIVE: There are saints who provide the Holy Sacraments (*makes a sign of the cross as if giving a blessing*).

SPEAKER SIX: There are saints who die for Jesus as a sign of faith (*slowly places one arm over the other on chest to symbolize dying*).

SPEAKER SEVEN: There are saints who simply sit in peace and think of the Lord (*places both hands, palm downward, on forehead as if praying*).

ST. JOHN: There are many saints. While on earth I saw a vision of the saint in heaven who sang, "With your blood you purchased for God people of every race and tongue, of every people and nation. You made out of them a kingdom and priests to serve our God." [Revelation 5:9-10]

ALL (*either speak or sing*): But, lo, there breaks
a yet more glorious day;
The saints triumphant rise in bright array;
The King of glory passes on his way. Alleluia, alleluia.

(*The seven exit from the direction from which they entered.*)

21.
November 3: Feast of St. Martin de Porres

Cast of characters:
    ST. MARTIN DE PORRES, dressed as a Dominican lay brother
    TOMAS, a lame layman
    BROTHER JUAN, another Dominican lay brother

Props needed: None

    (*ST. MARTIN de PORRES assists TOMAS, who limps to stage center from stage right.*)

ST. MARTIN (*speaking as they enter*): Señor Tomas, you are walking even better today.

TOMAS: I think so, too, Brother Martin. You are so kind to the poor and sick here in Lima. Until you started to help us, we were left to die in the streets.

ST. MARTIN: You give me too much credit, señor. I am only doing what the Lord calls us all to do. As Jesus said, "Blessed are they who show mercy; mercy shall be theirs."

TOMAS: The Lord indeed will bless you, Brother Martin. You are a very kind and merciful person.

    (*BROTHER JUAN enters from stage left.*)

BROTHER JUAN: Brother Martin, there are three more poor people at the door. Shall I send them away? We have no more room.

ST. MARTIN (*crossing to JUAN*): We can always find room for the poor. They can have my room.

BROTHER JUAN: But where will you sleep?

ST. MARTIN: I can sleep in the chapel. I feel close to God there.

TOMAS (*crosses to Juan*): Why don't you sleep in my room, Brother Martin? I'll sleep in the garden.

ST. MARTIN: No, Tomas. You need your bed. (*ST. MARTIN starts to move left with Tomas*) Let's go and welcome our friends who need us.

TOMAS and BROTHER JUAN: Blessed are you, Brother Martin. You are a friend to the poor and to everyone. (*During this speech TOMAS and BROTHER JUAN have moved to the far left of the stage with ST. MARTIN.*)

ST. MARTIN (*turning to them from the left*): And God has blessed me with good friends like you!

(*All three exit stage left.*)

22.
December 6: Feast of St. Nicholas

Cast of characters:
ST. NICHOLAS (best played by an adult or older student)
BOY ONE
BOY TWO
BOY THREE
GIRL ONE
GIRL TWO
GIRL THREE
TWO MORE CHILDREN, one boy and one girl

Props needed: None

Music: Tunes of "Jolly Old St. Nicholas" and "Jingle Bells"

(All eight CHILDREN enter: Four come stage right and four from stage left; all cross to stage center. At stage center they will sing special words to the tune of "Jolly Old St. Nicholas.")

CHILDREN (*singing*): Beloved old St. Nicholas, whose feast day is today,
We know that you help the poor more than words can say;
Little children love you now in a special way;
Beloved old St. Nicholas, come to us today.

(ST. NICHOLAS enters from stage right to stand in the middle of the CHILDREN. He should be dressed more like a bishop than Santa Claus. Perhaps ST. NICHOLAS could be seated on a stool with a child or two seated on his legs.)

ST. NICHOLAS: Children, what do you know about me?

GIRL ONE: Well, you were born in Turkey, Archbishop Nicholas.

GIRL TWO: And there are many legends about you. It's hard to know which ones are true.

BOY ONE: Some legends say that you like to give gifts. Why did you become such a giving person, St. Nicholas?

ST. NICHOLAS: I once saw a little child standing out in the cold, crying from hunger. I was told her parents had both died and she had no relatives. I started an orphanage so children without parents could have a home.

BOY TWO: Why do some people call you Santa Claus?

ST. NICHOLAS: In some parts of the world the name St. Nicholas was said slightly differently. My name became Santa Claus. I never wore a red suit and I was never very fat. But Santa Claus and I both love children and we both want to see them happy. We both want to help people who need help.

GIRL THREE: Santa Claus, I mean, St. Nicholas, can you sing a song with us?

ST. NICHOLAS: I'd like to sing with you. What shall we sing?

BOY THREE: We'll teach it to you. It's sung to the tune of "Jingle Bells."

CHILDREN (*singing*): Nicholas, Santa Claus, we should be like you:
Oh, how good it is to give in a loving, Christian way;
Let us all be friendly to those who are in need;
Our world will be a better place if Nicholas we heed.

(Santa or ST. NICHOLAS repeats the song with the children and then they exit in the same direction from which they entered.)

23.
December 12: Feast of Our Lady of Guadalupe

Cast of characters:
    MARY
    JUAN DIEGO

Props needed: Roses for MARY

Music: "Immaculate Mary" or other Marian hymn

> (*JUAN DIEGO, a poor Mexican Indian peasant, enters slowly from stage left and kneels.*)

JUAN: O God, I am a humble man. Thank you for converting me to the Catholic faith. Thank you for showing me how to live like Jesus. O Mary, Mother of God, pray for me.

> (*Slowly Juan sits back on his heels and seems to doze off. The choir could sing "Immaculate Mary" or another Marian hymn softly while MARY enters and stands above JUAN DIEGO. MARY holds some white roses—probably silk—under her mantle.*)

MARY (*speaking softly*): Juan—Juan Diego.

JUAN (*startled—he looks up but does not turn around immediately*): What? Who is speaking?

MARY: It is Mary. I heard you praying.

JUAN (*turning and bending over*): Mary, I am not worthy of your visit. Pray for me.

MARY: Juan, I would like a church built here at Guadalupe. Then people who travel here on pilgrimages will be able to pray to our Lord. Please tell the bishop that this is what I asked.

JUAN: O holy Mary, our bishop will never believe me.

MARY: Here, Juan, take these roses to the bishop. He will know I have spoken. Roses do not normally bloom in Guadalupe in December.

JUAN (*taking the roses*): Our Lady, I shall do as you request.

MARY: I shall put my picture on your cloak so that the bishop cannot fail to believe.

(*MARY turns and slowly exits stage right. JUAN DIEGO hurries off stage left.*)

24.
Feasts of Angels

Cast of characters:
  FOUR ANGELS
  FOUR SMALL CHILDREN: TWO BOYS and TWO GIRLS

Props needed: None

> *(The FOUR ANGELS enter: two from stage right and two from stage left; all four cross to stage center.)*

ALL ANGELS: One day God sent an angel to bring Mary the good news of human salvation. An angel watched over Mary and promised that the Holy Spirit would visit her and make her the mother of the savior.

> *(The FOUR CHILDREN enter and stand before the ANGELS.)*

CHILDREN: Angel of God, my guardian dear.

BOY ONE: What's a guardian?

GIRL ONE: You know, someone like Jane has—a person who cares for her in place of a mom and dad.

GIRL TWO: Angels can be protectors because they watch out for us.

BOY TWO: Each of us has an angel to watch out for us. We know a prayer for that angel.

ALL CHILDREN: Angel of God, my guardian dear, to whom God's love commits me here, ever this day be at my side to enlighten and guard, to rule and guide.

ALL ANGELS: We also bring messages from God.
We bring God's good news to people.

ANGEL ONE: The angel Gabriel gave Mary the news she was to be the mother of Jesus.

ANGEL TWO: An angel let Zechariah know that he and his wife,

Elizabeth, would be the parents of John the Baptist.

ANGEL THREE: Angels told shepherds that Jesus had been born in the stable at Bethlehem.

ANGEL FOUR: And angels gave the women at Jesus' tomb the news that he had risen.

ALL ANGELS: We angels praise God and watch over all God's children.

ALL CHILDREN: Dear guardian angel, ever this day be at my side to enlighten and guard, to rule and guide.

(All exit in the same direction as they entered. The CHILDREN exit first and then the ANGELS.)

25.
Feasts of Apostles

Cast of characters:
    JESUS
    SIX APOSTLES

Props needed: None

> (*JESUS enters from stage right with three of his APOSTLES. Three other APOSTLES enter from stage left and meet him at stage center. JESUS is speaking while he enters.*)

JESUS: There was a rich man who had a good harvest. "What shall I do?" he asked himself. "I have no place to store my harvest. I know!" he said. "I will pull down my grain bins and build larger ones. All my grains and my goods will go there." [Luke 12:16-20]

APOSTLE ONE (*the one who is to JESUS' immediate right*): Master, wasn't this a wise decision?

JESUS: Listen. I will tell you. The man thought he had blessings in reserve and grain stored for years to come. "Relax!" he told himself. But God said to him, "You fool! This very night your life shall be required of you. Who will own all this piled-up wealth of yours?"

APOSTLE TWO (*in group to the left*): James, you have my new tunic; I told you I wanted to wear it first.

APOSTLE THREE (James): (*the one to APOSTLE TWO's immediate left*) I won't let you eat the best cut of the lamb, John, if you won't let me wear your tunic.

JESUS: That is why I warn you, do not be concerned for your life, or what you'll eat. Don't be concerned about your body, or what you'll wear. Life is more important than food and the body is more than clothing. [Luke 12:22-26]

(JESUS moves past the APOSTLES to the left and turns back.)

Consider the ravens: They do not sow. They do not reap. They have neither cellar nor barn. But God feeds them. And you know how much more important you are than the birds.

(JESUS moves before the APOSTLES to the right as he speaks the following lines.)

Which of you by worrying can add a moment to your lifespan? If the smallest things are beyond your power, why be anxious about the rest?

APOSTLE FOUR: Lord, you speak wisely. I know we worry too much about everyday needs.

JESUS *(returning to center)*: Look at the lilies: They don't spin. They don't weave. But they are more splendid than King Solomon dressed in all his fine robes. If God clothes in such splendor the grasses of the field, which grow today and are thrown on the fire tomorrow, how much more will God provide for you! It isn't up to you to search for what you'll eat or drink. Stop worrying. The unbelievers of this world are always running after these things.

APOSTLE FIVE: I understand. God knows we need such things. If we ask God for them, the rest will follow in turn.

APOSTLE SIX: These words console me.

APOSTLE FOUR: I wonder who is first among us. [Luke 12:32-34]

APOSTLE TWO: I have a good claim because I was the first apostle chosen.

APOSTLE THREE *(shoves APOSTLE TWO)*: What do you mean? Jesus chose me before he picked you because I can preach to the crowds.

APOSTLE FIVE *(pulls APOSTLE THREE around to him)*: Who says you are a good preacher? I can preach better than you.

APOSTLE SIX: Lord Jesus, who *is* the first among us?

JESUS: The one who is the least!

APOSTLE ONE: What do you mean?

JESUS: Many that are first will be last and the last will be first. Don't live in fear, little flock. It has pleased God to give you everything you need. Sell what you have and give to the poor. Get purses for yourselves that do not wear out, a never-failing treasure with the Lord which no thief comes near nor any moth destroys. Wherever your treasure lies, there your heart will be. [Matthew 19:30; Luke 12:32-34]

APOSTLE SIX: God is love indeed and he who abides in love, abides in God. [1 John 4:16b]

ALL (*They turn forward as they speak. Insert apostle's name, in the possessive, for whom this feast is celebrated*):
_____'s faith was that of a true believer. The spirit of the Lord was upon him. The Lord anointed him. The Lord sent him to bring glad tidings to the poor, to proclaim freedom to captives, to recover sight for the blind and release for prisoners, to announce a year of favor from the Lord. [Adapted from Luke 4:18-19 and Isaiah 61:1-2]

(*JESUS and the three on the right exit stage right; the others exit stage left.*)

26.
The Ascension of the Lord

Cast of characters:
>   CHILD ONE
>   CHILD TWO
>   CHILD THREE
>   CHILD FOUR
>   CHILD FIVE
>   CHILD SIX

Props needed: Censer, three bouquets of spring flowers

>   (*THREE CHILDREN enter from stage right and THREE
>   CHILDREN enter from stage left to the center of the acting area.
>   CHILD TWO carries a censer while THREE CHILDREN each
>   carry a bouquet of spring flowers. The children should leave
>   enough space between them at the center so that the tabernacle or
>   cross area can be seen by the congregation.*)

ALL: Let the earth rejoice and let the angels sing, "Christ has
ascended on high."

CHILD ONE: Today Jesus the Lord ascended to heaven. (*CHILD
ONE crosses to a statue or picture of Jesus and places bouquet
before it.*)

ALL (*speaking slowly and with dignity as CHILD ONE completes the
above action*): Let the earth rejoice and let the angels sing,
"Christ has ascended on high." Sing to the Son of God as he
ascends on high above the clouds, alleluia.

CHILD TWO (*after CHILD ONE has returned to the group*): Today
Jesus rides on the heavens, the ancient heavens. He returns to
his home. (*CHILD TWO takes the censer and incenses the
tabernacle swinging the censer three times, each time in the sign of
the cross. Kneeling, CHILD TWO leaves the censer before the altar
for CHILD THREE and CHILD FOUR.*)

ALL (*speaking as CHILD TWO completes the above action*): Let the earth rejoice and let the angels sing, "Christ has ascended on high." Sing to the Son of God as he ascends on high above the clouds, alleluia.

CHILD THREE (*after CHILD TWO has returned*): When Jesus ascended on high, he showed us that we too can ascend to heaven. (*CHILD THREE places flowers before the tabernacle.*)

ALL (*speaking as CHILD THREE completes the above action*): Let the earth rejoice and let the angels sing, "Christ has ascended on high." Sing to the Son of God as he ascends on high above the clouds, alleluia.

CHILD FOUR (*after CHILD THREE has returned*): Let us realize that the spirit of Jesus is with us now and will be with us while the earth exists. (*CHILD FOUR goes before the tabernacle or cross and swings the censer three times in the sign of the cross and leaves the censer for CHILD FIVE.*)

ALL (*speaking as CHILD FOUR completes the above action*): Let the earth rejoice and let the angels sing, "Christ has ascended on high." Sing to the Son of God as he ascends on high above the clouds, alleluia.

CHILD FIVE (*after CHILD FOUR has returned to the group*): Jesus ascends to heaven. He has shown us the way to heaven while he was here on earth with his mother Mary. (*CHILD FIVE places flowers before a picture or statue of Mary.*)

ALL (*speaking as CHILD FIVE completes the above action*): Let the earth rejoice and let the angels sing, "Christ has ascended on high." Sing to the Son of God as he ascends on high above the clouds, alleluia.

CHILD SIX (*after CHILD FIVE has returned*): We are the sons and daughters of God and we also shall ascend to God in heaven. (*CHILD SIX goes before the tabernacle or cross and swings the censer three times in the sign of the cross and carries the censer back to the group.*)

ALL (*speaking as CHILD SIX completes the above action*): Let the earth rejoice and let the angels sing, "Christ has ascended on high." Sing to the Son of God as he ascends on high above the clouds, alleluia.

ALL (*speaking or singing after CHILD SIX has returned to the group*): Jesus Christ has ascended today, alleluia.

(*THREE CHILDREN turn and exit stage right. THREE CHILDREN turn and exit stage left.*)

27.
Feasts of Bishops

Cast of characters:
> BISHOP
> GIRL ONE
> GIRL TWO
> BOY ONE
> BOY TWO

Props needed: Bishop's miter (this hat could be formed from cardboard)
> Bishop's crosier or crook (shepherd's staff)

Music needed: "Like a Shepherd"

> *(The BISHOP enters from stage right and crosses to stage center. Immediately after him from stage right GIRLS ONE and TWO cross to the right of the BISHOP. BOYS ONE and TWO enter from stage left and cross to the BISHOP's left.)*

BISHOP: Anyone wishing to be first must become the servant of all.

BOY ONE: But, Bishop, you are our leader, not our servant.

GIRL ONE: You are the one who ordains and leads our priests.

BISHOP: Even the pope, our bishop of Rome, not only leads, but serves. A true leader is someone who thinks of the needs of all people in the community, just as a shepherd looks after his sheep.

GIRL TWO: Is that the reason why a bishop has a shepherd's crook?

BISHOP: Yes. This staff (*indicates crook*) is a sign of how the bishop is like a shepherd looking after a flock.

BOY TWO: The Bible calls Jesus "the good shepherd" because the people of ancient Israel knew that shepherds took care of their sheep.

BISHOP: Today the shepherd is still a good sign for a bishop. But today the people work *with* the bishop to carry out the work of the Church.

GIRL ONE: The bishop needs secretaries, lawyers, teachers, nurses, bankers, farmers, truck drivers and all kinds of people to help him carry out Christ's work on earth.

BOY ONE: (*name bishop for this feast*) _____ was that kind of bishop. He was a good shepherd, a leader of people.

(The following is an example of how a specific bishop could be worked into the play. Use a book about saints as a resource.)

GIRL TWO: Bishop Hilary, whom we honor this January 13, was born in France in the fourth century. After reading the Bible, he asked to be baptized.

BOY TWO: Bishop Hilary opposed the teaching of Arian, who said that Jesus Christ was not the Son of God. Bishop Hilary wrote very clearly about Jesus being the Son of God.

ALL: May Bishop Hilary, who was a teacher while on earth, now pray for us in heaven.

(Sing "Like a Shepherd" before the girls and bishop exit right and the boys exit left.)

28.
Christ the King

(Note: Christ the King is celebrated on the final Sunday of the Church year.)

Cast of characters:
    BOY ONE
    BOY TWO
    BOY THREE
    GIRL ONE
    GIRL TWO

Props needed: Table, if altar is not used
    Flower garland
    A gold crown made from cardboard

Music needed: "Crown Him With Many Crowns"

BOY ONE (*proclaiming to the congregation*): Christ is the King! Christ reigns forever! When Christ came to us, he taught us about the kingdom of God.

(*GIRLS ONE and TWO followed by BOYS TWO and THREE enter from stage left. They are also dressed in surplices and cassocks or in black and white street clothes. GIRL ONE carries a gold crown of cardboard.*)

ALL (*turn and speak forward*): Our Father, who art in heaven

GIRL TWO: hallowed be thy name.

GIRL ONE (*places the crown on the altar or table provided for this purpose at center; she then speaks*): Thy kingdom come;

GIRLS ONE and TWO (*together*): thy will be done on earth as it is in heaven.

BOY TWO: Give us this day our daily bread.

BOY ONE: Christ is the King! Christ reigns forever! When Christ came to us, he taught us how to ask for God's aid.

BOY THREE: Forgive us our trespasses as we forgive those who trespass against us.

BOYS TWO and THREE: And lead us not into temptation.

GIRLS ONE and TWO: But deliver us from evil.

BOY ONE: Christ is the King! Christ reigns forever!

> (*BOY ONE goes to the altar or table and lifts the crown above him, on high. He carries it above his head as he and GIRLS ONE and TWO, and BOY TWO and BOY THREE march down the center aisle or to the rear of the room while all sing, "Crown Him With Many Crowns."*)

29.
Feasts of Doctors of the Church

Cast of characters:
    GIRL SOLOIST
    BOY SOLOIST
    THREE BOYS
    THREE GIRLS

Props needed: None

Music: "Alleluia," except during Lent

> *(If the sanctuary has steps leading to the altar, FOUR CHILDREN can enter from stage right to form the vertical beam of a cross while TWO CHILDREN enter from stage right and TWO CHILDREN from stage left can form the horizontal beam. If, however, the sanctuary is flat and choir risers cannot be used, FOUR CHILDREN should enter from stage right and FOUR CHILDREN from stage left to form a semicircle in front of or around the altar.)*

ALL: A doctor of the Church is a person who is devoted to the study of God's law, who explores the wisdom of the people of old and who interprets the prophecies. [Sirach 39:1-10]

GIRLS: This child of God treasures (*hands to hearts*) the speeches (*cupped gesture of right hand coming from mouth forward*) of wise people and studies difficult sayings.

BOYS: This person studies mysterious stories (*unraveling an imaginary scroll with right hand while holding the bottom of the scroll with the left*) and tries to figure out what wise people have said.

GIRL SOLOIST: The doctor is considered to be a great thinker and is able to speak with leaders of nations.

BOY SOLOIST: The doctor travels among the peoples of foreign lands to learn what is good and evil (*extends hands outward as if to include the congregation*).

ALL: The doctor's job is to seek (*all hands are extended upward as if asking favors of the Lord*) the Lord, to ask favors from God (*hands down*), to open lips in prayer (*right hands to mouth*), to ask pardon (*right hands strike breasts*) for sins (*drop hands to sides*).

GIRLS: If it pleases God, (*mention the saint's name*) _____ will be able to understand many things.

BOYS: (*mention the name of the saint*) _____ will speak wise words and give thanks to the Lord in prayer.

ALL: Who will direct (*mention the saint's name*) _____'s knowledge and wisdom while meditating on the Lord's mysteries? (*All place both hands on their foreheads.*)

GIRL SOLOIST: Many will praise (*mention the saint's name*) _____'s understanding.

BOY SOLOIST: (*mention the saint's name*) _____'s work can never be forgotten.

ALL: People will speak of (*mention the saint's name*) _____'s wisdom and together will sing [his, her] praises.

(*All lead the congregation in singing an "Alleluia," except during Lent. FOUR CHILDREN exit stage right and FOUR CHILDREN exit stage left.*)

30.
Easter Sunday: The Resurrection I

[Based on Matthew 28:1-10, Mark 16:1-8, Luke 24:1-12 and John 20:1-10]

Cast of characters: ANGEL
    MARY ONE
    MARY TWO
    MARY THREE
    JOHN
    PETER, who is older than JOHN

Props needed: A symbol of Christ's empty tomb—such as a white cloth draped over a table. Abandoned wrappings or another symbol can also be devised.

Music needed: A joyful song appropriate for Easter to be played at the beginning and end of the play

(*The ANGEL comes to stage center. The ANGEL stands to the right of the tomb symbol. The three MARYS enter from stage left. They cross to below the ANGEL and just to the ANGEL's left.*)

ANGEL: Whom are you seeking?

MARY ONE: We seek Jesus of Nazareth who was buried here.

ANGEL: He is not here; he has risen from the dead.

MARY TWO: What do you mean?

ANGEL: Remember what Jesus said to you while he was still in Galilee? The Son of Man must be delivered into the hands of sinful men and be crucified...

MARY THREE (*as if remembering, she finishes the ANGEL's sentence*): ...and on the third day rise again!

ANGEL (*gestures to the empty tomb*): See the place where he was laid?

MARY TWO: It is empty, as you say.

ANGEL: Go quickly and tell his disciples: The Lord has risen from the dead. He now goes ahead of you to Galilee, where you shall see him. This is the message I have for you.

(*The ANGEL exits stage right.*)

MARYS ONE and TWO (*They turn to each other and say together*): Glory be to God in heaven and on earth. Praise to our Lord, Jesus Christ, the Son of God.

MARY ONE: Let us hurry to tell the disciples.

MARY TWO: Peter especially will want to know.

(*JOHN comes running on from stage right.*)

MARY THREE: Here is John. Perhaps he has already heard.

JOHN: Heard what?

MARY TWO: An angel spoke to us and said the Lord has risen from the dead as he predicted.

MARY ONE (*She goes up to the tomb while the other women stay on the left.*): See, the tomb is empty. Only the burial cloth remains.

JOHN (*falls on his knees*): Praise be the Lord, our Savior Jesus Christ!

PETER (*rushes on from stage right*): John, I couldn't keep up with you. What's going on here?

JOHN (*He stands.*): Peter, the Lord has risen!

MARY TWO: An angel told us he has risen and the tomb is empty.

MARY THREE: The angel also said that our Lord will go before us to Galilee where we will see him.

PETER: This is truly the day the Lord has made!

JOHN and the three MARYS: Let us be glad and rejoice!

PETER: Come! We must go to Galilee now and prepare for the arrival of our Lord!

(*PETER leads JOHN and the three MARYS off left. Joyful Easter music could accompany their exit.*)

31.
Easter Sunday: The Resurrection II

[Matthew 28:1-10]

Cast of characters:
FIRST MARY
SECOND MARY
ANGEL
JESUS

Props needed: The tomb can be represented by a large box with a door cut in it up center in the staging area. The doors are closed. The TWO MARYS enter from left and cross halfway to the tomb.

FIRST MARY (*turning to the other Mary*): How can we anoint the body of Jesus if we can't enter his tomb?

SECOND MARY: But who will be able to roll the stone away? (*A large drum roll or recorded clap of thunder is heard and the two MARYS kneel. The angel, who can simply wear a white alb, enters from right and walks slowly and with dignity to stand to right of tabernacle or representation of tomb. The two MARYS turn to each other in fright after the angel stops moving.*)

ANGEL: Don't be afraid! I know you are seeking Jesus who was crucified. He isn't here. He has risen just as he predicted. Come and see the place where he lay. (*The ANGEL opens the door or tabernacle or tomb and both MARYS cross to the left side of it.*)

FIRST MARY (*turning to the SECOND MARY*): It's empty!

ANGEL: Jesus has risen from the dead. He's going before you into Galilee. You'll see Jesus there. Walk quickly and tell his disciples what you've heard and seen.

(*The MARYS cross to their original position at left center while the ANGEL exits slowly right.*)

SECOND MARY: This is a wonderful day!

FIRST MARY (*continuing*): Glory be to the Father and to the Son and to the Holy Spirit.

JESUS (*quietly*): Mary, Mary. (*They move a step or two to the right in surprise.*) Don't be afraid.

FIRST MARY (*crossing before the SECOND MARY to JESUS*): Lord, we're so happy that you're alive!

JESUS: I haven't ascended yet to God so you must not touch me.

SECOND MARY (*crossing behind FIRST MARY*): Jesus, you've proved you are the Son of God by rising from the dead.

JESUS: Go and tell my followers to go to Galilee. There they will see me.

MARYS (*quietly together*): Yes, Lord.

(*JESUS watches the MARYS exit left. He then kneels and extends his hands upward.*)

JESUS: God, I will tell everyone how great you are once more before I go to heaven to be with you.

(*As JESUS slowly lowers hands and stands, joyful Easter music is sung or played. JESUS exits slowly left in the same direction as the MARYS.*)

32.
Feasts of Martyrs

Cast of characters:
  MALE SOLOIST ONE (BOY or MAN)
  MALE SOLOIST TWO (BOY or MAN)
  ONE BOY or MAN
  FEMALE SOLOIST ONE (GIRL or WOMAN)
  FEMALE SOLOIST TWO (GIRL or WOMAN)
  ONE GIRL or WOMAN

Props needed: None

  (*The THREE MALES and THREE FEMALES come on in groups from stage right and stage left, respectively. They should wear neutral, flowing clothing: choir robes, cassocks or albs of some type. They stand as two groups at center right and center left in triangles.*)

MALES (*slowly lifting hands to where they are clasped together above their heads into an inverted V*): Hear us, Lord. Listen to our call for help. [Psalm 17:1-2]

FEMALES (*also slowly lifting hands to a clasped position above their heads*): Hear our prayer from lips that don't lie.

ALL (*hands remaining together above their heads*): Let our decisions come from you. Your eyes see what is right.

  (*All hands come slowly down to sides.*)

FEMALE SOLOIST ONE: These are the people who have survived the great period of trial; they have washed their robes and made them white in the blood of the lamb. [Revelation 7:14]

FEMALES (*crossing their hands and placing them over their hearts*): You test our hearts. You search them in the night. (*hands, still crossed with palms up, extended forward*) You try us with fire. (*turn palms down, pass hands over each other in a sweeping motion on "won't"*) But you won't find any ill will in us. (*Hands pointed to, but not covering, mouths—slowly shake heads negatively*) We haven't told lies as people often do; (*open arms wide in an affirmative gesture*) we have obeyed your laws. [Psalm 17:3-4]

MALES (*one step forward on "always"*): Our steps have been always in your paths. (*Shake heads slowly back and forth as if to say "no."*) Our feet have not tripped. [Psalm 17:5]

MALE SOLOIST ONE: It was this that brought them before God's throne:
day and night they minister to him in his temple:
he who sits on the throne will give them shelter. [Revelation 7:15]

FEMALE SOLOIST ONE (*stepping forward*): I will call upon you, for you will answer me, O God: (*lifting her arms toward heaven, palms extended*) Incline your ears to me; hear my word. Show your wondrous kindness, O savior of those who flee from their foe to safety at your right hand. [Psalm 17:6-7] (*Lowers arms and steps back into triangle.*)

MALE SOLOIST ONE (*stepping forward*): Keep me as the apple of your eye. (*crossing arms before him with palms facing himself as if avoiding light*) Hide me in the shadow of your wings from the wicked who use violence against me. [Psalm 17:8-9]

(*The other TWO MEN and THREE WOMEN slowly encircle the MALE SOLOIST. The same MALE SOLOIST continues.*)

MALE SOLOIST (*arms outstretched before him as if to protect himself*): Cruel enemies beset me; they shut their mean hearts; their mouths speak proudly. Their steps even now surround me (*Those in the circle crouch to their knees. The MALE SOLOIST leads the others into a straight line facing the congregation.*) like lions hungry for food, like young lions lurking in hiding. [Psalm 17:10-12]

FEMALE SOLOIST (*stepping forward with her right hand upward*): Rise, O Lord, (*gestures with fist flung downward on "cast"*) cast them down! Rescue me by your sword from the wicked. [Psalm

17:13] (*She steps back in line.*)

ALL: By your hand, O Lord, from mortal men,
from mortal men whose only interest is in this world. [Psalm 17:14]

MALE SOLOIST ONE (*taking one step forward*): These are the ones who have survived the great period of trial. [Revelation 7:14]

FEMALE SOLOIST ONE (*taking one step forward*): They have washed their robes and made them white in the blood of the lamb. (*MALE and FEMALE SOLOISTS ONE exit stage right and stage left, respectively.*)

MALE SOLOIST TWO (*taking one step forward*): Never again shall they know hunger or thirst,

FEMALE SOLOIST TWO (*taking one step forward*): nor shall the sun or its heat beat down upon them, for the Lamb on the throne shall shepherd them. [Revelation 7:16-17] (*MALE and FEMALE SOLOISTS TWO exit stage right and stage left, respectively.*)

Remaining MALE and FEMALE SOLOISTS speak together: He will lead them to springs of life-giving water
and God will wipe every tear from their eyes. [Revelation 7:17]

(*These two exit stage right and stage left, respectively.*)

33.
Feasts of Our Blessed Mother Mary

[Note: See the calendar for specific dates.]

Cast of characters:
    MARY
    THREE GIRLS DRESSED IN WHITE
    THREE BOYS DRESSED IN BLUE

Props needed: None

Music: Marian hymn such as "Immaculate Mary," "Hail, Holy Queen Enthroned Above," "Hail Mary: Gentle Woman," "My Soul Rejoices," "Sing of Mary," "Be Joyful, Mary," "Blessed Mary/Ave Maria," "Mary, Full of Grace" or other hymn.

(THREE GIRLS enter from stage right to center and THREE BOYS enter from stage left to center. After all have entered into a semicircular arrangement, they speak. All movements are slowly executed and there are noticeable pauses between phrases.)

ALL (*raising hands toward heaven*): Hail Mary (*pause*)

(*blessing themselves slowly*) full of grace (*pause*)

(*right hands to hearts*) the Lord is with you. (*pause*) [Luke 1:28]

(*crossing arms before them*) Blessed are you among women

SOLOIST: and blessed is the fruit of your womb, Jesus.

ALL (*as if cradling baby in arms, gently sway arms*): Holy Mary, mother of God (*pause*)

(*MARY enters slowly from stage right and stands in center space between THREE GIRLS right and THREE BOYS left.*)

ALL (*after MARY is in position, they kneel toward her*): pray for us sinners, (*pause*) now (*pause*) and at the hour of our death. Amen.

MARY: My soul proclaims the greatness of the Lord;
My spirit finds joy in God my savior. [Luke 1:46-47]

ALL (*continuing to kneel*): Remember, most gracious Virgin Mary,
that never was it known that anyone who fled to your
protection, asked your help or sought your aid was left unaided.

MARY: For he has looked upon his servant in her lowliness;
all ages to come shall call me blessed. [Luke 1:48]

ALL (*except MARY*): Inspired with this confidence, we fly to you, our
Mother; to you do we come, before you we stand, sinful and
sorrowful.

O Mother of the Word made flesh, despise not our petitions,
but in your mercy hear and answer us.

MARY: God who is mighty has done great things for me,
holy is his name. [Luke 1:49]

ALL (*repeated*): O Mother of the Son of God, despise not our
petitions, but in your mercy, hear and answer us.

(*MARY and the others kneel toward the tabernacle. The choir
and/or congregation sing a Marian hymn. After the hymn is sung,
all stand. MARY leads the GIRLS on the right off stage right while
the BOYS on the left turn and exit stage left.*)

34.
Feasts of Pastors

Cast of characters:
    FOUR DISCIPLES
    ST. PAUL

Props needed: None

Music needed: "They'll Know We Are Christians"

> (*FOUR DISCIPLES enter: two come from stage right, two from stage left. They stand at stage center.*)

DISCIPLES: I will give you shepherds after my own heart. They will teach you knowledge (*right hands to foreheads*) and wisdom (*hands to heart and then down at their sides*).

> (*As the DISCIPLES speak, PAUL enters to stage center to stand behind and between the two pairs of DISCIPLES.*)

DISCIPLE ONE: Paul summoned the priests of the Church at Ephesus.

PAUL (*speaking to the DISCIPLES*): Keep watch over yourselves and over the whole flock the Holy Spirit has given you to guard. Shepherd the Church of God, which was acquired at the price of Jesus' own blood. I recommend that you know the Lord and that gracious word which can help you grow and give you a share among all the people of God. You need to recall the words of the Lord Jesus who said:

DISCIPLES: "There is more happiness in giving (*extend right hands, palms open, as if giving*) than in receiving" (*extend left hands, palms closed as if taking*). [Acts 20:17-36]

DISCIPLE TWO: After this speech, Paul knelt down with them and prayed. (*All kneel.*)

DISCIPLES: It should be clear to all that Father (*insert pastor's *name*) _____ is Christ's servant, explainer of the mysteries of God.

PAUL (*stands*): The great quality of a pastor is to be faithful to his duty.

ALL: The great quality of a pastor is to be faithful to his duty.

(*The choir and/or the congregation sing "They'll Know We Are Christians." PAUL exits with the DISCIPLES on the right to stage right and the two remaining DISCIPLES, on the left, exit stage left.*)

35.
Pentecost

Cast of characters:
> THREE GIRLS

Props needed: None

Music needed: "Come, Holy Ghost" or other hymn to the Holy Spirit

> *(THREE GIRLS enter from stage right. They kneel in a line before the tabernacle or the cross on the center table briefly, then they stand and turn toward the congregation.)*

GIRLS: Lord, send out your Spirit and renew the face of the earth.

GIRL ONE (*crossing down to stage left*): The Spirit of the Lord came upon Mary and the apostles and they could understand many languages and speak in many tongues.

GIRLS: Lord, send out your Spirit and renew the face of the earth.

GIRL TWO (*crossing down to stage right*): The Spirit of God is one with the Father and the Son. The Spirit gives us many blessings and helps us understand God's will.

GIRLS: Lord, send out your Spirit and renew the face of the earth.

GIRL THREE (*crossing down to stage center*): All who are chosen by the Spirit of God are the daughters and sons of God. We have been adopted by God to share in God's kingdom.

GIRLS: Lord, send out your Spirit and renew the face of the earth.

> *(The GIRLS at stage right and stage left join the GIRL at stage center to form a circle.)*

GIRLS (*as they walk in a slow circle three times*): Come, Holy Spirit; come, fill our hearts with love; come, help us to know God's ways and desires. (*They may repeat this sentence if necessary to make the words last through three circles.*)

(When finished, the GIRLS leave as the congregation joins in singing a hymn to the Holy Spirit.)

36.
Feasts of Popes

Cast of characters:
    JESUS
    PETER
    SIX APOSTLES

Props needed: None

Music needed: "The Church's One Foundation"

> (*JESUS enters from stage right with PETER following. They cross to stage center.*)

JESUS (*speaking as they cross*): To you, Peter, I shall give the keys of the kingdom of heaven. (*THREE APOSTLES enter stage left and THREE enter stage right as JESUS and PETER arrive at stage center.*) Whatever you will bind upon the earth will be bound also in heaven and whatever you will forgive upon the earth will be forgiven also in heaven. [Adaptation of Matthew 16:19]

PETER: Lord, you mean that I shall lead our people?

JESUS: You are Peter and so I shall build my Church upon this rock. [Matthew 16:18]

ALL APOSTLES: The rock is our master, Jesus Christ, and upon this foundation even Peter himself was raised.

> (*The APOSTLES form a V-shape with JESUS and PETER as the apex.*)

TWO APOSTLES CLOSEST TO AUDIENCE: Built on a rock the Church does stand.

FOUR APOSTLES CLOSEST TO AUDIENCE: Even when worldly kingdoms are falling.

ALL SIX APOSTLES: Jesus, our Lord, will help our band

JESUS and PETER and the SIX APOSTLES: to stand for love as our calling.

ALL: Lord, you chose (*insert pope's name for this feast*) _____ as pope of your Church to protect the faith and lead us in worship.

PETER: Help us to be witnesses to your truth, Lord,

ALL: and be strong supporters of our Church community today.

> (*All sing "The Church's One Foundation" or some other appropriate song. PETER and THREE APOSTLES who entered stage right exit stage right. JESUS and OTHER APOSTLES exit stage left.*)

37.
Feasts of Religious or Holy Persons

Cast of characters:
  THREE GIRLS
  THREE BOYS

Props needed: None

(*THREE GIRLS enter stage right; THREE BOYS enter stage left. Once they have a formed a semicircle or a V-shape at stage center, they speak.*)

ALL: There is nothing colder than a Christian who does not seek to save others.

GIRLS: You cannot plead poverty.

GIRL SOLOIST: The widow putting in her two small coins will be your accuser.

BOYS: You cannot plead humble birth.

BOY SOLOIST: Saints Peter and Paul were humbly born, of humble stock.

ALL: You cannot plead ill health. Many of the saints were frequently ill.

(*The BOYS mime being trees by putting their arms in a circle above their heads.*)

GIRLS: Look at the trees that do not bear products. Have you not noticed how strong and fine they are, upstanding smooth and tall? (*The BOYS lower their arms.*)

(*The GIRLS mime being trees that have products by raising their arms above their heads as if they are holding bowls in their hands.*)

BOYS: If we had a garden, we would much prefer trees with products—oranges and olives—to those that have none and are only for pleasure. (*GIRLS lower arms.*)

ALL: Such are those people who think only of their own needs and desires. In fact, they are even worse than the trees without products. The trees, at least, can be used for building or protection.

(*The BOYS extend their arms upward to the sun while the GIRLS speak.*)

GIRLS: If you say that the sun cannot shine, you have insulted God.

(*The BOYS lower their arms. The GIRLS extend their arms forward as if offering gifts.*)

BOYS: If you say that a Christian cannot help others, you have insulted God.

ALL: It is easier for the sun not to shine than for the Christian not to shed light.

(*Insert name below of religious or holy person.*)

ALL: _____ is the light of the Lord and lived as a child of light. Light produces every kind of goodness (*all use their hands to form heart shapes*) and justice (*all hold their right hands upward, palms open, as if taking an oath*) and truth (*all cross their left arms over their right arms on their chests*).

(*After a pause, the BOYS exit stage left and the GIRLS exit stage right.*)

38.
Sacred Heart of Jesus; October 16: Feast of St. Margaret Mary Alacoque

[Note: The Sacred Heart of Jesus is celebrated on the Friday after Corpus Christi Sunday.]

Cast of characters:
    ST. MARGARET MARY ALACOQUE
    FOUR CHILDREN

Props needed: A picture of the Sacred Heart
    An easel if the altar is not used

Music: A hymn to the Sacred Heart

    (*ST. MARGARET MARY ALACOQUE, carrying a picture of the Sacred Heart, enters from stage right. FOUR CHILDREN enter from stage left. They sing the first verse of a hymn to the Sacred Heart as ST. MARGARET MARY ALACOQUE places the picture of the Sacred Heart on the altar or an easel at stage center. She kneels at stage center after she has placed the picture and the FOUR CHILDREN complete the song.*)

ST. MARGARET MARY: Lord, you gave me a vision of your Sacred Heart. I believe that you love us with all your heart.

CHILDREN: O, Sacred Heart, you give us peace and you help us bring peace to others.

ST. MARGARET MARY: Lord, your heart sends us three things. The first is a stream of sorrow for our sins and a firm desire to overcome our faults.

CHILDREN: O, Sacred Heart, you give us sorrow and a desire to correct our sinful natures.

ST. MARGARET MARY: Lord, your heart sends us charity to help us all overcome the obstacles that keep us from being truly holy.

CHILDREN: O, Sacred Heart, you give us your charity that forgives our weaknesses and helps us overcome them.

ST. MARGARET MARY: Lord, your heart sends us love and light to help us be one with you.

CHILDREN: O, Sacred Heart, you give us your love and light that help us know you and unite ourselves to you.

(ST. MARGARET MARY joins the children at left and they all sing a final verse of the hymn to the Sacred Heart. They then turn left and exit.)

39.
Feasts of Virgins

Cast of characters:
SEVEN GIRLS INCLUDING ONE SOLOIST
GOD (voice over public address system)

Props needed: None

Music needed: "Faith of Our Fathers" or "Holy, Holy, Holy"

(*SEVEN GIRLS enter: Four come from stage right; three from stage left. They form a V-shape with the soloist at the apex.*)

ALL: The unmarried woman is concerned with things of the Lord, in pursuit of holiness in body and spirit. [1 Corinthians 7:34]

SOLOIST (*raising hands above her with palms together as if in prayer*): The Lord is my leader; this I know in my heart (*right hand to heart and then down by her side*).

ALL: Come, daughters, draw close to the Lord, and share the splendor of his light (*Add "Alleluia" during the Paschal or Easter season*).

SOLOIST: If we compare the Church to a tree (*extends her arms wide above her as branches*), unmarried women are its blossoms (*she forms a circle with her right hand's thumb and index finger*). [Sermon by St. Cyprian, bishop and martyr]

ALL: They are the image of God that reflects the holiness of the Lord.

SOLOIST: St. Catherine of Siena speaks for holy women when she says, "I have tasted and seen the depth of your mystery and the beauty of your creation with the light of my understanding. I have clothed myself with your likeness and seen what I shall be."

ALL: "Eternal God, you have given me a share in your power and the wisdom that Christ claims as his own, and your Holy Spirit has given me the desire to love you." [*Dialogue on Divine Providence* by St. Catherine of Siena]

GOD (*voice over public address*): My daughters, you are enriched with the gift of the Holy Spirit and cleansed of all sin by the shedding of Christ's blood.

ALL: We shall go forth from the quiet of prayer to bear witness to the truth of the Lord.

(*"Faith of Our Fathers" or "Holy, Holy, Holy" is sung. The GIRLS exit in the same direction from which they entered.*)

Resources for Music

The following books are excellent sources for locating the songs recommended for use in these plays.

Breaking Bread Seasonal Issue with Annual Music Issue, ed. John J. Limb. Portland, Oregon: Oregon Catholic Press, updated annually.

Glory & Praise, Volumes 1 and 2. Phoenix, Arizona: North American Liturgy Resources, 1977.

Hymnal for Catholic Students. Chicago: Liturgy Training Publications and G.I.A. Publications, 1988.

The ICEL Resource Collection. Chicago: G.I.A. Publications, 1981.

Young People's Glory & Praise, Volumes 1 and 2. Phoenix, Arizona: North American Liturgy Resources, 1984, 1991.